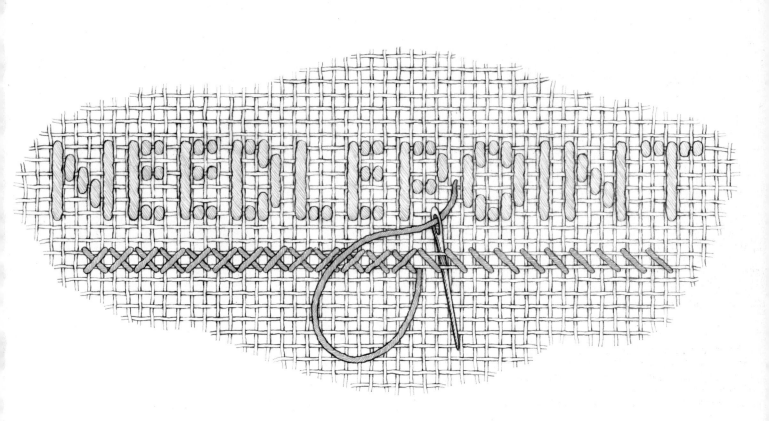

NEEDLEPOINT

SARAH WINDRUM

TREASURE
PRESS

CONTENTS

Notes for American Readers
Throughout this book, the American term (where it differs from the British one) is given in square brackets. American readers should refer to the colour guide on page 78 when buying yarns to make the projects in this book.

First published in Great Britain in 1980 by
Octopus Books Limited

This edition published in 1987 by
Treasure Press
59 Grosvenor Street
London W1

© 1980 Octopus Books Limited

ISBN 1 85051 225 6

Printed in Hong Kong

INTRODUCTION

The craft of needlepoint – or canvas embroidery – has flourished in Europe since the early 16th century and in America since colonial times. It is often referred to as tapestry, because of the resemblance of some needlepoint stitches to this type of weaving.

History

Embroidery in general developed in many parts of the world soon after the invention of plain sewing. It branched into two main types: free-flowing stitching worked on closely woven fabrics and a more geometric type of stitching which follows the grid of open-weave materials. Canvaswork developed from this second variety; the shape and size of the stitches being determined to a large extent by the grid of the material on which they are worked. Within this limitation many hundreds of stitch patterns and types of design are possible; one is by no means limited to geometric designs.

Unlike other forms of geometric stitching on open-weave materials, such as the cross-stitch embroidery of Scandinavia, needlepoint normally involves completely covering the ground with yarn. Each stitch fortifies the background material, so that – particularly when tent stitch or cross stitch is used – a very strong, textured fabric is produced. This is very suitable for articles which will receive a lot of wear, such as upholstered chairs or cushions [pillows], and covering such items has traditionally been one of the main uses of needlepoint.

19th century stitch samplers worked in Berlin wools.

Early 20th century purse worked in silks and metal threads.

THE ORIGINS OF NEEDLEPOINT

The word 'canvas' comes from the Greek *kannabis*, meaning 'hemp'. Although it is an ancient material, there is no real evidence of canvas being widely used as an embroidery ground until the 16th century. However, similar types of embroidery on even-weave fabrics were practised by the Romans and the Anglo-Saxons, and it seems that almost every culture in the world has independently developed traditions of embroidery based on this concept.

The oldest known surviving examples of needlepoint are some fragments of a ribbon stole worked in plait stitch, the ground of which has entirely disintegrated, leaving only the silk yarn. Estimated to be pre-13th century, they were unearthed in the 19th century when the tomb of Archbishop Hubert Walter at Canterbury Cathedral was opened.

OPUS ANGLICANUM

By the 13th century the English had developed a distinctive and beautiful type of embroidery. As with all art forms in Europe during the Middle Ages, the work was almost entirely of an ecclesiastical nature. Known as Opus Anglicanum (English work), it used rich, luxurious fabrics as grounds for couched gold threads, seed pearls, semi-precious stones and marvellously ornate stitching. Many of the borders were worked in needlepoint. The work was greatly prized by the Church; in 1295 the Vatican was known to possess more Opus Anglicanum than any other kind of embroidery. The work was appreciated not only for its artistic merit but also for its precious materials, which made it a good financial investment. Many fine examples still exist, among them the famous Syon Cope in the Victoria and Albert Museum in London. The entire surface of this magnificent cloak is covered with embroidery, including stitches characteristic of free-style embroidery, such as split stitch and couching, as well as geometric stitches – cross and plait stitch. The work depicts scenes from the life of Christ.

In another case nearby is displayed the Hildesheim Cope. Made in Lower Saxony in the early 14th century, it shows the influence of Opus Anglicanum and uses coloured silks and gold threads worked in brick stitch and couching. The interlocking circular motifs represent the martyrdom of saints in gory detail, and wherever the motifs intersect there is a little dragon. Opus Anglicanum declined towards the end of the 14th century, and thereafter ecclesiastical embroidery as a whole suffered a great reduction in quality, becoming stereotyped and unexciting. Recurrent wars and political disruptions, along with the drastic loss of population caused by the Black Death, contributed to this decline.

DEVELOPMENTS IN THE 16TH CENTURY

It was not until the 16th century that needlepoint became widely practised, and even then its potential as a craft in its own right was not recognized. Large woven tapestries depicting grand classical and biblical scenes had become popular as wallhangings in large houses. Such tapestries were expensive, due to the high labour costs and the complicated machinery needed to produce them. It was then discovered that a variation of tent stitch, called rep(s) stitch, could produce detail comparable to that in tapestry and a similar ridged effect. The relative simplicity of this technique and its avoidance of cumbersome and costly machinery meant that it could be used in private households. Many copies of woven hangings were made in this way, and many of these embroidered 'tapestries' have outlasted the originals.

This introduction of needlepoint into domestic use stimulated the interest of English ladies of leisure, and during the reign of Elizabeth I – herself a keen embroiderer – the creative potential of the craft began to be recognized. It then acquired the essentially intimate nature that it has retained to this day. Needlepoint achieved immense popularity as a pastime, and large households engaged professional embroiderers to adapt and produce designs for the lady of the house to work, often assisted by her servants. Many of the designs had a personal quality, depicting autobiographical scenes, almost like a diary, and canvaswork from this period has a delightful freshness and fascination. The Elizabethans revelled in embroidery and enthusiastically began to decorate everything in sight. Canvaswork was particularly popular as it is so hardwearing. It appeared frequently on the cushions that substituted for upholstery in those days. Wallhangings, bed hangings, handbags, bookbindings and table and floor carpets were also embroidered with needlepoint. The craft was rapidly growing and acquiring new stitches, of which Turkey work (a tufted stitch that imitates rug pile) was particularly popular.

The Oxburgh Hangings

The Oxburgh Hangings are a charming and beautiful example of the technical devices and little motifs employed by the Elizabethans. They were made by Mary Queen of Scots and Elizabeth, Countess of Shrewsbury (later known as Bess of Hardwick), during the Queen's long imprisonment in England under the surveillance of the Earl of Shrewsbury. Mary and Bess, both accomplished needlewomen, spent many hours working together on embroideries. The Oxburgh Hangings are made of green velvet, embellished with appliquéd panels of tent and cross stitch worked in silk with some gold thread. These needlepoint motifs are engagingly naive, depicting extraordinarily conceived little animals, such as 'a Tiger' and 'a Frogge', which bear scant resemblance to their living counterparts. The work also includes brief mottoes, and each of the hangings has a larger central scene. One of these shows a beautiful, stylized marine fantasy, complete with an octopus and a seahorse with hooves and a mermaid tail. The borders contain coats of arms and heraldic devices. Originally there were four hangings, but one of these was later cut up to make bed curtains and a valance.

The Bradford Table Carpet

Another magnificent example from the late 16th century is the Bradford Table Carpet, worked in tent stitch using silk thread on

'Woodpecker' wallhanging designed by William Morris and woven at Merton Abbey, Surrey, in 1885.

very fine canvas. The centre of the carpet has a repeating motif of a fruiting vine on trelliswork, but it is the wide border that contains the really extraordinary and beautiful work. About 38 centimetres (15 inches) deep, it presents a continuous panorama of English country life in fascinating detail. Although made during the Renaissance, it echoes the characteristic medieval disregard for perspective. Trees bearing enormous leaves and acorns overshadow tiny stylized houses and castles; a lion pursues a naked man who is climbing a tree, and hunters and fishermen go about their business among diverse flora and fauna, ponds, rivers and bridges, all treated with the same charming naivety.

PATTERN BOOKS AND STITCH SAMPLERS

In the late 16th century, printed pattern books began to appear, along with embroidery slips. These were intricate cut-out shapes, usually of flowers, birds and trees, which could be embroidered and then applied to a fabric ground. Metal needles became more widely available, replacing those of bone and ivory – another factor contributing to the ever-increasing popularity of all kinds of embroidery. The earliest known dated stitch sampler was produced in 1598; it was stitched by Jane Bostocke and inscribed: 'Alice Lee was borne the 23 of November being Tuesday in the afternoone 1596'. The stitches are in metal and silk thread on linen and form many complex patterns. Various other samplers from this period have survived; these were mainly experimental or reference works not intended for display.

BARGELLO WORK

The popularity of canvaswork increased enormously, reaching its height in the late 17th century. Chairs were now commonly upholstered and canvaswork provided the ideal material. An extensive variety of stitches was now in use. One of the most popular styles for upholstery was bargello – also known as Florentine work and Hungarian point. One superb example of bargello is the bed hangings at Parham Park in Sussex, England, which are worked in shades of gold, brown and beige. The origins of bargello are obscure, but it seems likely that it came from Hungary to Florence, where it acquired the names 'Florentine' and 'bargello' (possibly after the Bargello Palace in that city).

DECORATIVE EMBROIDERY

From the mid-17th century onwards there was more emphasis on purely decorative embroidery, either framed or hung on walls, and put to no practical purpose. The Hatton Garden Hangings in the Victoria and Albert Museum are a very good example of the pictorial work done in the second half of the century. Consisting of six panels, each 2.75 by 1.30 metres (9 by 4 feet), they were embroidered with wool on relatively coarse canvas. The stitches include tent, cross, brick, rococo, croslet, French knots and some couched work. Fabulous giant flowers are depicted, entwined around carved pillars – a typical motif of this period, which preferred large exuberant blooms to the delicate English honeysuckles, roses and herbs of the Elizabethans. At the lower edge of the panels are the customary bizarre miniature animals: lion, leopard, dragon, camel, elephant, unicorn and horse. Higher in the panel there are many exotic birds.

A strong oriental influence was apparent by the 18th century, with chinoiserie dominating. Professional embroiderers set up shops throughout Europe, selling materials and kits, and the personal element in design to a large extent disappeared with this commercialization of the craft. Persian carpet patterns were also widely admired and emulated.

NEEDLEPOINT STYLES IN THE UNITED STATES

By the end of the 18th century canvaswork was declining in popularity in Europe, while at the same time – thanks to the importing of suitable materials – it was becoming popular in America. The early Americans were keen needlewomen, especially fond of crewel embroidery and patchwork quilt making. Several cultural traditions were represented in North America, and styles and techniques from Germany, Holland and France, as well as Britain, contributed to American needlework. Indian motifs often found their way into patchwork designs. However, the Americans remained untouched by the Eastern influence that had swept Europe, and their canvaswork remained essentially domestic in character.

BERLIN WORK

In the mid-1800s Berlin wool work became extremely fashionable in both Britain and America. It was so called because the wools

Right: 16th century English needlepoint cushion cover.

and patterns were imported from Berlin, where, in 1835, a German painter and his wife had devised a method of reproducing patterns in colour. Although printed patterns had been produced as early as the 16th century, they were in monochrome. Coloured patterns were a great innovation and made things very easy for the embroiderer. The designs tended to be vulgar and sentimental, using bright, even garish, colours. The earliest pieces were worked on fine silk canvas, which was available in many colours and manufactured at least until the 1880s. The background was often left unworked, which made the motif stand out from the surface. True Berlin wool work is almost completely confined to the 19th century, when it was so popular that it usurped other types of needlework for many years. The growth of a relatively affluent and leisured middle class furthered its popularity.

DYES AND FABRICS

Until the mid-19th century wools were coloured with natural dyes, which are very fast. Many remain unfaded even today, and where some discoloration has occurred, it tends to be fairly even throughout the colour range.

Aniline dyes (gas colours) were invented and patented by Sir William Perkin in 1856 and first manufactured in 1858. The first colour obtained was purple, followed by a large range of colours, some of which were very gaudy – a factor that contributed to the garishness of much of the subsequent work. At first the mordants (fixing agents) used were the same as for vegetable dyes, and since these were unsuitable, aniline dyes faded quickly and unevenly, the red/blue shift being particularly unstable.

A greater variety of fabrics was now used. Besides the traditional even-weave cotton and linen and silk, one could buy canvas made of jute or wool. Fine wire mesh and even perforated cardboard were also in evidence. Cardboard was bought in sheets with regularly spaced pre-punched holes. It was mainly used for simple texts in England, although in America more imaginative and elaborate pictures were embroidered on this unlikely material.

THE VICTORIAN ERA

The Victorians decorated every available surface in their homes, and embroidery was a favourite means of embellishment. Needlepoint bell-pulls, bags, spectacle cases, screens, fire-screens, pictures, slippers and tea-cosies competed for attention with needlepoint chairs, cushions and carpets. Towards the end of Queen Victoria's reign the industrial revolution was beginning to be felt in the world of embroidery. Machine-embroidered fabrics were commonly available by the turn of the century. It was in reaction to such mass-produced work in all the decorative arts and the mawkishness of Victorian taste that the Arts and Crafts Movement developed under the leadership of William Morris. Morris and his disciples produced hand-made furnishings of elegant design and fine workmanship. Inspired by their work, a group of embroiderers calling themselves 'Art Needlework' began, during the 1870s, to raise the quality of embroidery design. Apart from some new designs, including a return to geometry, they made copies of 17th century works using faded yarns to simulate ageing. Art Needlework was applauded by the art world and the critics, who had been emphatic in their disapproval of contemporary excesses. Later, the fluid lines of *art nouveau* were interpreted in needlework, again to critical praise and encouragement. There followed a period of growth and integration of interior and exterior design, in a united attempt by architects, designers and craftsmen to reintroduce aesthetic integrity into the decorative arts. This movement was a great success, and fabrics, wallpaper and furniture, as well as embroidery, once again acquired elegance and dignity. The London store Liberty's, founded in the early 1800s, provided a showplace for the new art, particularly the designs of William Morris and his followers.

THE 20TH CENTURY

Needlepoint, along with other kinds of embroidery, again suffered a decline after the first two decades of the 20th century. This may have been due to rapid developments in fabric-printing techniques which enabled even fairly complex designs to be

Wallhanging designed by William Morris, 1898.

reproduced efficiently and cheaply and so filled the need for pattern in interior design.

There was a brief resurgence of interest in needlepoint in the 1930s, when it was among the crafts that attracted the attention of the Bloomsbury Group and the London School of painters, who were again attempting to integrate the arts and crafts. Duncan Grant and Vanessa Bell, in particular, designed several pieces. A needlepoint pole screen from that same period was among the exhibits at the Victoria and Albert Museum in 1932 in the museum's 'Exhibition of Modern Embroidery'. Designed by the painter Anthony Betts, it showed how practitioners of the fine arts were beginning to descend from their pedestals and to recognize the potential of this and other crafts.

MODERN TRENDS

There was, however, little further activity or innovation in canvaswork until the 1950s and 60s, when embroidery underwent perhaps the most radical transformation in its history. It was a time of great upheaval in the visual arts, and traditions were ruthlessly discarded in the search for new and more immediate means of self-expression. This increased freedom, however, was often accompanied by carelessness of execution and the use of bizarre materials – machine waste, eggboxes and the like – which had little to offer apart from their shock value. Today, such extremes are apparently dying a natural death, and we are left with some real gains – notably the greatly expanded repertoire of stitches, which have brought more exciting textures into needlepoint. Many designers are exploiting these textures in most imaginative ways in abstract compositions that have great sensuous impact. Pictorial embroidery, too, is enjoying a renaissance as designers bring new interpretations and techniques to traditional subjects.

Among the various kinds of embroidery being practised today – crewel, ecclesiastical, drawn thread work and others – needlepoint is easily the most popular. In the United States, in particular, it is being enthusiastically taken up by thousands of people – including men – who had scarcely ever before held a needle and thread. Undoubtedly there are many reasons for its popularity, one being the tactile pleasure of handling the materials and another being the rhythmic, soothing quality of the work itself. Also, of course, it is a practical form of embroidery, useful for upholstery and other furnishings as well as for personal accessories. The appeal of decorative, functional and hand-made objects is stronger than ever in a world increasingly dominated by machines.

For the serious embroiderer today the opportunities are virtually unlimited. The liberating influence of the 1960s and increased knowledge of the skills and visual languages of other cultures have opened up countless avenues for creativity. The embroiderer, like other modern craftsmen, can adapt and learn from the achievements of all ages and traditions.

MATERIALS AND EQUIPMENT

The materials needed for needlepoint are simple. The basic requirements are canvas, yarn and a needle. You will also need equipment for transferring the design to the canvas and for stretching [blocking] the finished piece. An embroidery frame, though not essential, may also be useful.

CANVAS

Any material with an even grid can be used – even wire mesh – but the canvas made specifically for needlepoint is usually of cotton or linen. It is manufactured in a variety of widths, 90 cm (36 in) being the standard width for most types; but some canvases are available up to 152 cm (60 in) wide. There are two main types: single thread (mono) and double thread (penelope) canvas.

Single canvas consists of an even grid of horizontal and vertical threads and is graded according to the number of threads per inch. (So far, metrication has not been applied to the system of grading canvas.) It is normally loosely woven and frays easily, but there is also an interlock type, in which the warp and weft threads are actually woven through each other. Double canvas is constructed differently, in that each vertical and horizontal 'thread' consists of two strands. The paired strands of the warp (those running parallel to the selvedge) are usually placed close together, whereas there is a little more space between the pairs of weft strands. Double canvas is sometimes graded, for clarity, according to holes per inch, rather than threads (because the threads are double). We shall normally use the term 'gauge' in referring to both single and double canvas. Thus, 14-gauge single canvas has 14 threads to the inch, and 14-gauge double canvas has 14 pairs of threads (28 strands) to the inch.

Which canvas to use

Single canvas is easier to use and will take all the stitches, so is probably the better choice for the beginner. However, double canvas does have some advantages. For instance, when using straight stitches you can insert the needle between paired horizontal threads occasionally to give a smoother line on a curve. Also, you can intersperse areas of smaller stitches by first spreading the paired warp and weft threads into an even grid by pushing a large needle into the intersections. Twenty stitches to the inch, instead of 10, can then be worked on 10-gauge double canvas. If the work is to be trammed before stitching (that is, padded with horizontal threads), then double canvas is required.

The very coarse rug canvases are all in double weave. Double canvas is widely available in gauges ranging from three to 20. Single canvas is to be found in the range of 10 to 22 and sometimes even finer.

When working in straight stitch, it is usually best to use either single canvas of the interlock type, or double, rather than ordinary mono canvas. This is because a stitch going over only one thread can easily slip sideways under the single warp thread during the stretching [blocking] process. (Single straight stitches are best used sparingly, as they do not cover the canvas adequately.)

Buying canvas

When buying canvas, check to see that there are no knots or breaks in the threads and that these are smooth, evenly spaced and not too skewed. Poor quality canvas often has very rough threads, and it is sized after it has been woven. This makes it rather stiff, and the size rubs off on the hands while you work. Better quality canvases are slightly softer, as less size is used and the threads are polished to make them smooth before weaving.

It is well worth the money to use the best materials throughout for such a painstaking craft. Good materials are not only a pleasure to work with but also long-lasting.

Canvas colours vary, the most usual being white, yellow, beige and brown. The colour to use is really a matter of personal choice, as the background will not normally show through on the finished work. Some people prefer to use white canvas, as the yarn colours show more clearly on it during the stitching. On the other hand, it can be tiring to the eyes, particularly in the finer gauges.

YARN

Many different kinds of yarn can be used, and different types can be mixed in one piece of work.

Wools

The basic and most useful yarns are tapestry wool, crewel wool and Persian wool – which is widely available in the United States but only now becoming available in Britain. All three kinds of wool are very hardwearing and are usually mothproofed. Crewel is a very fine wool, which can be used as a single strand or with several strands combined. Persian wool is slightly thicker, but can also be used on a wide range of canvases by varying the number of strands used. Tapestry wool is relatively thick and is used as a single strand, which makes it less flexible. It is suitable for medium-gauge canvas, particularly 14-gauge.

The thickness of yarn required will vary according to the gauge of canvas and the type of stitch being worked. Straight stitches usually require a slightly thicker thread on any given gauge of canvas than do diagonal stitches. On 14-gauge canvas, one strand of tapestry wool, two strands of Persian, or three strands of crewel is sufficient for tent stitch, whereas brick stitch will require four strands of crewel or a tapestry and a crewel together. For most diagonal stitches, six crewels will adequately cover 7-gauge double canvas.

With most yarns the dyelots do vary a little, so if you are using a large quantity of a particular colour it is advisable to calculate the amount you will need and allow a little extra. As a rough guide, a 13.5 m (15 yd) skein of tapestry wool will cover about 25.5 sq cm (10 sq in) in tent stitch on 12-gauge canvas.

Other embroidery threads

In addition to embroidery wools, any reasonably strong and even thread can be used, including embroidery cottons, silks and metal threads. Some knitting yarns are also suitable, but make sure to select those which are strong, reasonably smooth and not too elastic. If you use a very elastic yarn, it will be difficult to maintain even tension, and the canvas will become greatly distorted.

Silk is very effective but rather expensive, so is perhaps best reserved for highlights at first. Metal threads are difficult to use; they tend to kink and to slip through the needle, but they can be used for details. Perhaps the easiest way to use them is as embellishments, couching them onto already stitched canvas-work. (To couch a thread, lay it on top of the work in the desired position; then, using a finer thread, secure it in place with tiny stitches spaced about 1 cm [½ in] apart.)

Most embroidery and knitting wools are colourfast, but all yarns should be tested for this before use, as the dyes may run in the stretching [blocking] process.

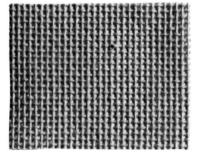

*single canvas
18 threads to the inch*

*double canvas
12 holes to the inch*

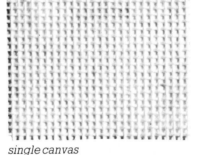

*single canvas
16 threads to the inch*

*double canvas
10 holes to the inch*

*single canvas
14 threads to the inch*

*double canvas
8 holes to the inch*

*single canvas
12 threads to the inch*

*double canvas
5 holes to the inch*

NEEDLES

Tapestry needles are blunt and have a long eye to accommodate the relatively thick threads used. Sharp needles are not suitable, as they tend to split both the wool and the canvas threads, slowing down the work. Tapestry needles are manufactured in a range of sizes; the higher the number, the finer the needle.

Choose a needle that will accommodate the wool comfortably. The yarn will slip around in too large an eye and be frayed by one that is too small. The needle should also be able to pass smoothly between the canvas threads without pushing them aside.

Needles become rough and discoloured after a while. When this happens, try cleaning them with wire wool [steel wool], but if this is unsuccessful, throw them away, or they will spoil your work.

FRAMES

A frame is not essential, but it does have some advantages. It prevents distortion of the canvas by holding it taut. An adjustable frame (as opposed to a plain stretcher frame) also makes the work easier and more comfortable by holding the canvas at a convenient height and angle. Also, if you are stitching a large piece, such as a heavy rug or wallhanging, the frame will take the strain off your arms.

The method of working with a frame is a little different from that used without one. When working without a frame you can make each stitch in a single movement, pushing the needle in to complete one stitch and bringing it through to start the next at the same time. If the canvas is stretched tautly over a frame then each stitch must be made in two movements, passing the needle through from one hand to the other. This two-handed method is somewhat slower.

Commercial frames

Special needlepoint frames can be bought in a variety of sizes and styles, but the basic make-up of each is the same: two horizontal rollers, each covered with webbing or tape, slot or screw into wooden side laths. The top and bottom edges of the canvas are sewn onto the tapes, and the sides laced around the laths. The best type is the free-standing, adjustable floor frame. Table frames with stands can also be adjusted to a comfortable working angle.

To attach the canvas to the frame, first sew the top and bottom edges to the tapes, working outwards from the centre and keeping the canvas taut. Then lace the sides to the frame, using fine string or button thread.

Making your own frame

If you prefer, you can use a simple stretcher frame. This can easily be constructed from four pieces of wood nailed together, or from picture stretchers, which slot together at the corners and are held firm by wooden wedges. The frame must be strong enough to take the strain of the taut canvas, which should be attached with drawing pins [thumbtacks] as follows: pin the centre of one side, then the centre of the opposite side, then the centre of the third and fourth sides. Next, secure the four corners, keeping the canvas taut and the threads square. Then fill in the sides with drawing pins [thumbtacks], taking care not to split any threads, until the canvas is evenly stretched and taut like a drumskin.

OTHER TOOLS

To prepare the design and transfer it onto canvas

Tracing paper; plain white paper; graph paper; a black pen; a ruler; a set square [right angle]; sticky [cellophane] tape; a waterproof pen and/or waterproof inks or coloured markers (the finished embroidery will be dampened in the stretching [blocking] process).

To prepare the canvas

A large pair of scissors for cutting the canvas; cotton thread or tape to bind raw edges; fine string or button thread for lacing canvas to frame; drawing pins [thumbtacks] if using a stretcher frame.

To work the embroidery

A pair of sharp-pointed scissors for cutting yarn and unpicking (dissecting scissors are excellent for this purpose); a thimble (useful if working without a frame and 'sewing' the stitches).

To stretch [block] the finished work

A large sheet of white or brown paper; a ruler; a set square [right angle]; a black waterproof pen; a sponge, cloth or spray for dampening the work; a board somewhat larger than the canvas, such as hardboard [particle board] or plywood; wallpaper paste and a 6–12 mm ($\frac{1}{4}$–$\frac{1}{2}$ in) brush.

WORKING CONDITIONS

Finally, a word about working conditions. It is important to have very good light, especially when stitching on fine canvas and when selecting colours. A comfortable working position is also essential, and it does help greatly to have a clean and tidy working area with yarns laid out neatly and tools within easy reach.

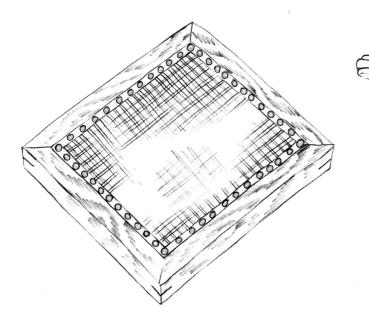

STITCHES

In the next few pages you will find some of the most popular of the many needlepoint stitches. Some, such as Scottish stitch, are really combinations of other stitches. Many such combinations can be devised, and by mixing two or more shades in one stitch you can produce completely new patterns. This selection is intended to show the basic flat stitches and some of those patterns most suited to the nature of the ground material.

The diagrams show the best method of working each stitch. These methods are worked with an easy, flowing movement, usually giving long stitches on the back of the canvas. It is not a good idea to economize on yarn by working so as to make a short stitch crossing only one thread on the underside. This feels awkward, and it also twists the wool in such a way that the stitches are formed badly on the front and the canvas shows through, giving an untidy appearance and a weaker fabric.

The first diagram shows tramé, which is a method of laying in the design with horizontal threads, which are then worked over, usually in tent stitch. Tramming gives extra bulk and firmness to the stitches and is used principally for upholstery and rugs.

The basic and most often used needlepoint stitch is tent stitch. It is the finest stitch that can be worked on any given gauge of canvas and is therefore the best for outlines and fine detail and one of the most useful in pictorial representation. When worked on very fine canvas it is often called petit point; worked on coarse canvas it is called gros point.

If you do have difficulty in working out how to stitch curves, try drawing some on graph paper and filling in the squares that are crossed by the lines. Let each square represent a tent stitch, and work this pattern on the canvas.

Graph paper is also useful if you want to rescale a stitch pattern or invent a new one.

TRAMÉ
For this method, a thin strand is worked between the horizontal threads of double canvas. Do not lay threads more than 7.5 cm (3 in) long, and work so that there is as little thread as possible on the back of the canvas. Long threads on the front and excess wool on the back will snag the yarn when you do the stitching.

This modern stitch sampler is worked in silk threads on single canvas. Parts of the canvas have been purposely left unworked and an occasional glass bead sewn onto the unworked areas.

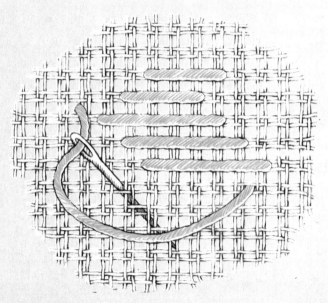

14

TENT (CONTINENTAL)

This is the method of working tent stitch used for details and outlines. It produces a long, oblique stitch on the back which makes a strong fabric, but it tends to distort the canvas considerably and so is less useful than basketweave tent (see below). All stitches should slant in the same direction.

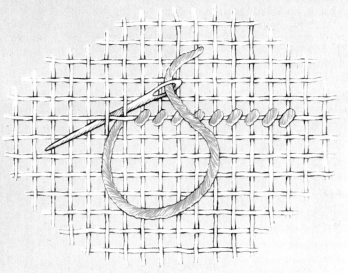

TENT (BASKETWEAVE)

This method of working tent stitch is the best for large areas and should be used wherever possible. A smoother surface is produced and the shape of the canvas is distorted less because the stitching on the back is vertical and horizontal rather than oblique. The name 'basketweave' refers to the effect produced on the underside of the work.

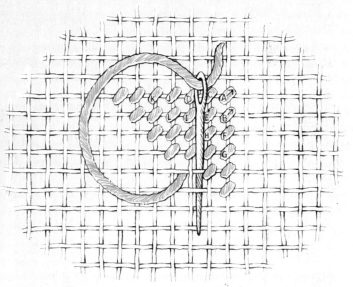

STRAIGHT

Although it follows the canvas grid, this stitch – worked in a random pattern – has a free-flowing quality which makes it particularly suitable for shading effects and blending colours. It is very quick to work. Stitches can be made over any number of threads but should be staggered, as the canvas will show where two adjacent stitches end on the same level.

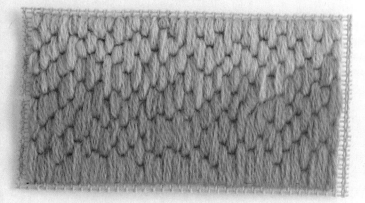

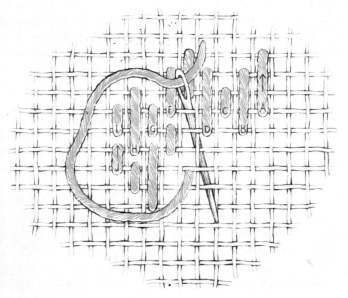

BRICK

This is a useful background stitch. Its textural appearance is similar to straight stitch, though more regular, and it also works well in mixed colours. It can be rescaled, but must be worked over an even number of threads. As with any straight stitch, it can be worked horizontally or vertically.

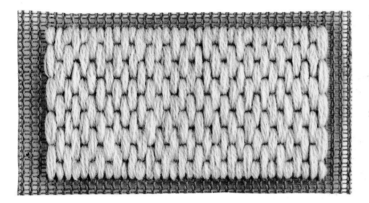

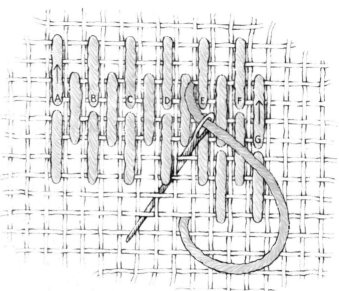

UPRIGHT GOBELIN

This stitch is hardwearing and suitable for upholstery if trammed. It can easily be rescaled – that is, worked over three or four threads instead of two. You can see that the threads show through slightly between the rows, and this should be borne in mind when choosing canvas colour. The stitch is named after Gobelin tapestries, which it imitates.

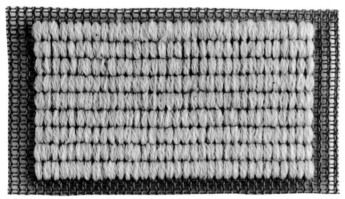

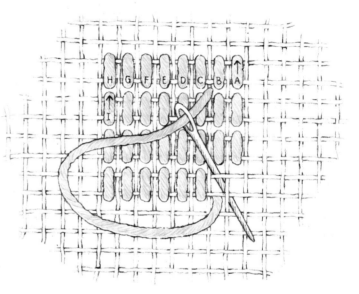

ENCROACHING GOBELIN

This is another very good stitch for shading effects. Try working a sky in a range of shades, working gradually down from medium blue to pale grey. This stitch has to be worked carefully, as it distorts the canvas, making it difficult to stretch back into shape, particularly if used alongside other stitches.

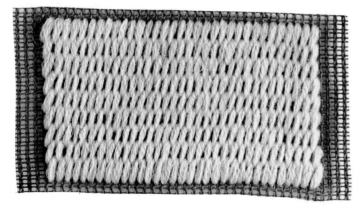

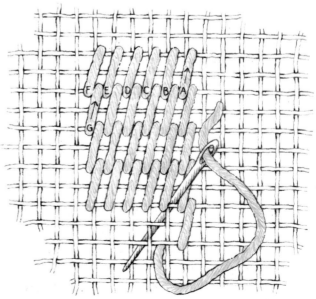

CROSS

This very hardwearing stitch is often used for upholstery and especially for church kneelers. It is useful for geometric designs and backgrounds but difficult to use in naturalistic designs because of its particular texture and the difficulty of following curves. It should be worked with all the top stitches slanting in the same direction.

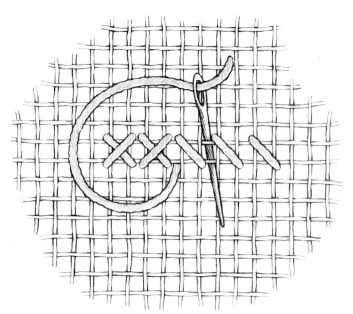

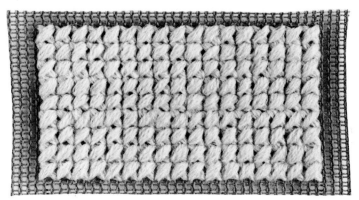

UPRIGHT CROSS

This is a strong, highly textured stitch. The limitations are similar to those of cross stitch. It is normally worked with all the top stitches either vertical or horizontal, but an interesting effect can be produced by alternating vertical and horizontal top stitches.

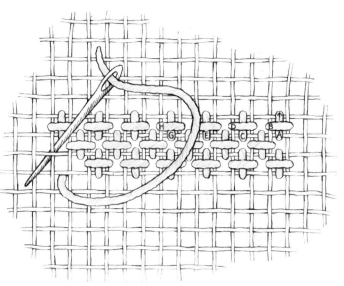

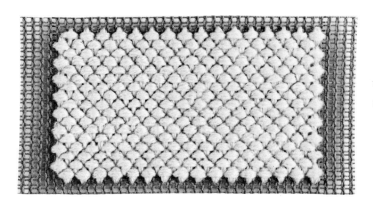

SATIN

This is an extremely versatile stitch which gives a sheen and lightens the colours. The width of the rows can be varied, as can the number of stitches in a row. It is worked in horizontal and vertical rows, slanting in either direction.

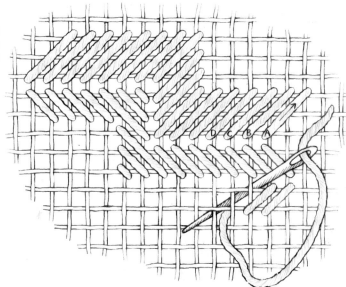

SQUARE MOSAIC (CUSHION)

Worked in one colour, this stitch catches the light to produce interesting textural effects. Using two or more colours can produce quite different patterns. For instance, you can make a patchwork effect by working groups of stitches in different colours.

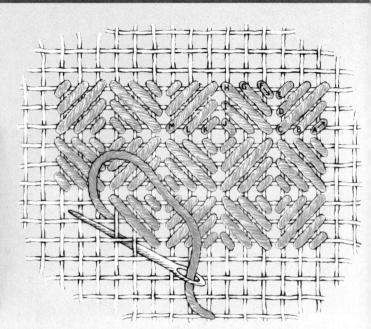

DIAGONAL MOSAIC (1)

This is a very simple flat stitch that nevertheless gives a strong textural effect and a marked diagonal pattern which show up well even in a small area. Like any diagonal stitch that slants in only one direction, it is technically very easy to combine with tent stitch.

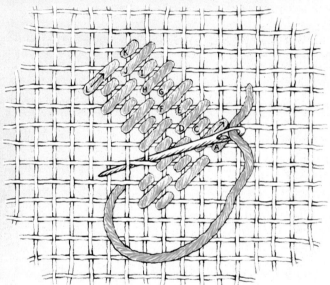

DIAGONAL MOSAIC (2)

This is simply a rescaled version of diagonal mosaic (1). Interesting variations can be produced by using more than one colour. For example, you can make a stylized floral pattern by working the hexagonal shape made by a ring of six groups in one colour and the group in the centre in another colour – both colours contrasting with the background.

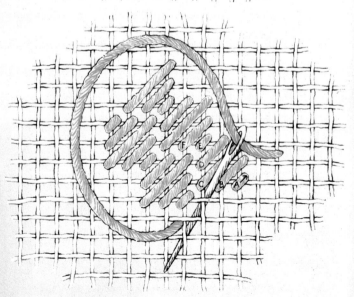

HUNGARIAN POINT (BARGELLO, FLORENTINE WORK)

Once the first line is worked the rest follow fairly automatically, but you must make sure that you put the right length of stitch on top of the 'peaks'. You will see, if you follow a vertical line of stitches, that there is a regular pattern of two short then two long stitches.

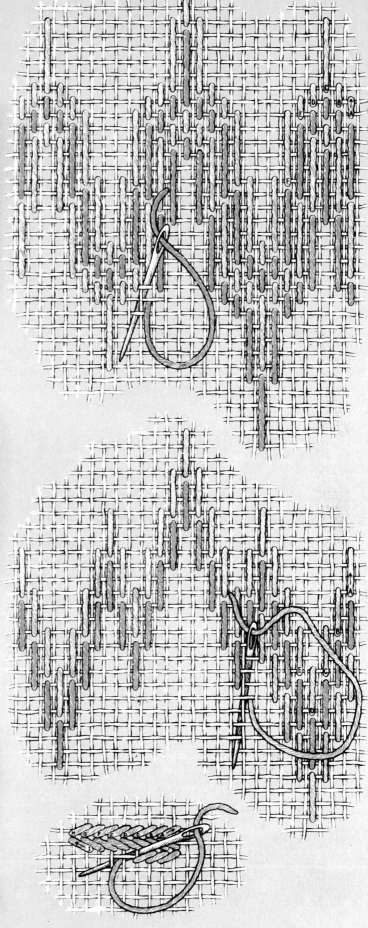

FLORENTINE FLAME

This stitch is similar to Hungarian point but uses only one length of stitch and so is somewhat easier to work. Like Hungarian point, it needs to be worked over a large area in order to develop the design fully, and its bold pattern is difficult to mix with other stitches.

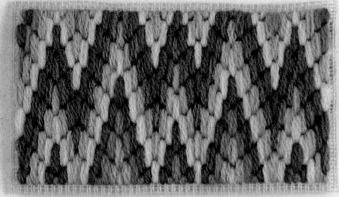

KELIM (KNITTING STITCH)

This is a strong, close stitch which resembles stocking stitch in knitting. It can be worked in either horizontal or vertical rows. Because of its oblique angles it is difficult to fit into a smooth outline, and care must be taken to cover the canvas where it meets other stitches.

LEAF

Many quite different patterns can be formed with this stitch by using two or more colours. For example, the stitches that cross at right angles can be worked in a second colour to form a lattice; or the lower stitches in each group can be worked in one colour and the top ones in a lighter tone.

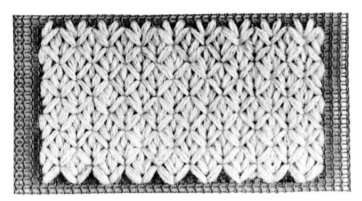

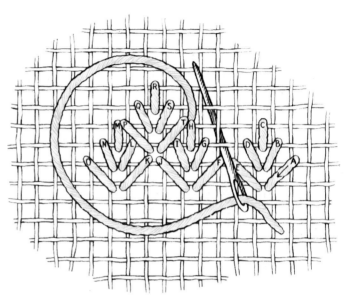

LATTICE (1)

This simple lattice pattern is best worked in two tones. Any degree of contrast can be used. If worked in pale colours it has a lacy appearance. Using two contrasting tones gives a three-dimensional effect. The stitch can easily be rescaled.

LATTICE (2)

This is a more complex lattice, usually worked in three colours, but more or less can be used. It has the appearance of large-scale basketweave. If contrasting colours are used a three-dimensional effect is produced. Very different spatial illusions can be achieved by varying the placement of the colours. (The letters show the order of working in one colour.)

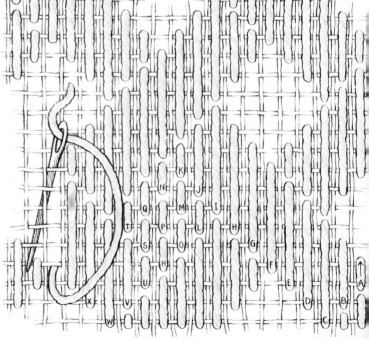

STAGGERED GRID PATTERN

This stitch needs a fairly large area in order to develop the pattern fully. Work the tent stitch grid first, then the square, then the ray filling. As with all patterns containing oblique stitches, the edge may have to be altered when meeting other stitches. For example, if the point formed by the ray would cut into a curved area of tent stitch, the ray stitches could be eliminated and tent stitch substituted over that part of the grid.

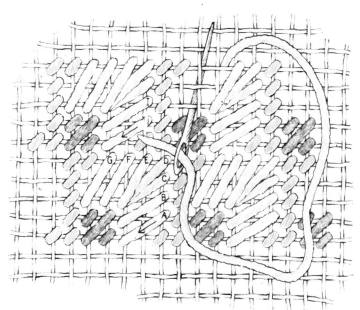

SCOTTISH

This is a combination of tent and mosaic, usually worked in two colours. It is easiest to work the complete tent stitch grid before the squares. To vary the pattern you could slant the mosaic in the opposite direction to the tent stitches, or you could alternate their direction as in square mosaic. The stitch can easily be rescaled by altering the size of the squares.

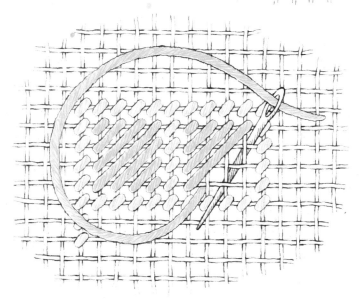

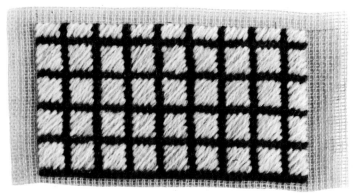

WEAVING

This stitch has a woven appearance, though the yarns are not actually woven through each other but worked in alternating blocks of horizontal and vertical straight stitches. The illusion of weaving can be strengthened by working the vertical and horizontal blocks in two different colours.

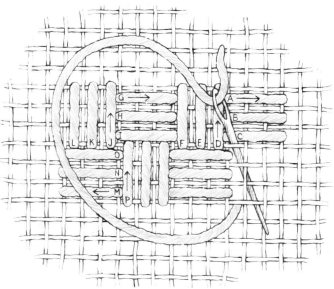

DESIGN

Design has been defined as the process by which order is created out of chaos – or, in the arts and crafts, as conscious arrangement of shape and colour. Although one can formulate general rules of design, the characteristics of the materials in any particular craft impose certain limitations, as well as offering certain possibilities. Good design in any art or craft exploits the intrinsic potential of the materials and is sympathetic to them. What may work in a painting, for example, may not work in needlepoint, and vice versa.

Adapting a design for needlepoint

The sheep picture opposite was taken from a relatively unsuccessful watercolour and is a very good example of how a basically sound design that lacks magic as a painting can acquire harmony and beauty when translated into wool. When I came to adapt this particular design for needlepoint, it became obvious that the tree on the left of the painting would have to go; for although in the watercolour it was just acceptable, in embroidery it would have overwhelmed the other elements, including the low key colours that give the scene its mood and charm. The simple design relies entirely on the subtly changing colours for its impact. Although many needlepoint designs use intricate pictorial elements or a variety of decorative stitches, these are by no means essential, as you can see. This kind of embroidery can produce lovely atmospheric effects simply by the skilful mixing of different shades of wool. The border was extremely difficult to conceive, for although the picture needed some kind of decorative edge, every colour I tried initially overpowered the misty light in the scene and washed out the colour. The colours finally chosen pick out the warm areas in the picture without detracting from the cool distances.

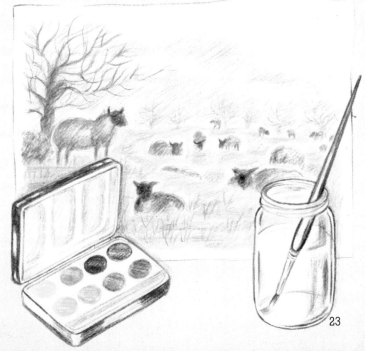

UNSUITABLE DESIGNS

There is little point in putting all the time and effort required for needlepoint into a subject that would be more appropriate in another medium. Compared with some other textile crafts, needlepoint is very labour intensive, and because it lacks the immediacy of painting, for example, you cannot rely on spontaneity to introduce visual interest and freshness into your work. In many arts and crafts one can obtain beautiful effects by exploiting the occasional accident – paint running to produce unexpectedly beautiful patterns or ceramic glazes separating and forming lovely colours; but the sensuous qualities of wool are very different from those of paint or dye; also unlike them, it lacks the ability to record the physical energy of its application. With canvaswork any exciting developments that happen on the way are not produced by the materials themselves but by your own understanding and insight as the work progresses.

You might, for example, feel tempted to copy a large abstract painting consisting of broad areas of luscious and luminous colour, but this sort of work owes its success entirely to the qualities of the medium and the artist's exploitation of them. Think carefully before transposing any design that consists mainly of flat areas of colour; ask yourself if the design will benefit from the textural qualities of canvaswork. Probably one of the best criteria to apply is that if it is boring to work it will be equally boring to look at – and large areas of tent stitch in one colour are *very* boring to work!

FIRST THINGS FIRST

Before starting to design from scratch, it is a good idea to learn the basic skills of the craft. As you become more familiar with both the limitations and the potential of the materials, you will find that workable and exciting ideas will suggest themselves. Begin by making a sampler, perhaps, then use the projects in this book to develop technical proficiency and acquire a 'feel' for the craft.

PLANNING AN ORIGINAL DESIGN

One of the first points to consider when you do embark on an original design is the use to which the finished article will be put. How hardwearing does it need to be? If it is to be used as a chair seat or rug, for example, it is going to receive a great deal of wear, so one of the more durable stitches, such as tent or cross stitch, should be used. If it is to be a purely decorative article, such as a wallhanging, then you are at liberty to choose stitches purely for their aesthetic qualities. When designing a piece for a particular setting, you must also carefully consider the colour and style of the decor. You may want the cushion [pillow] or hanging to blend harmoniously with the setting; or you may prefer the work to contrast boldly with it. Or perhaps the contrast will be of a more subtle kind. Select a range of colours in sympathy with the existing colours of the room, and throughout the planning and execution of the piece compare it with other fabrics, shapes and colours with which it is to be displayed, ensuring at each stage that your design will harmonize rather than clash with them. Working within these limitations will increase your command of the medium and stretch your creative abilities.

UPHOLSTERY

Early in the design process you will need to decide on the dimensions and shape of the piece. If it is intended for upholstery you would be wise to get a professional upholsterer to make a template for you and then to work to it very accurately.

Needlepoint for upholstery has two intrinsic design problems. First, you must remember that the finished work will not be perfectly flat – in some cases it will be very curved. Also, the shape may not be rectangular; chair seats, for example, are often trapezoidal. So you must try to think three-dimensionally in positioning the design elements and try to complement the shape

within which you are working. Look at historical examples to see how these problems have been successfully resolved. You will find beautiful examples in museums and art galleries all over the world. Secondly, the design must be consistent with the structural rhythms of the article to be covered. If it is a period piece, you would do well to study illustrated books on the arts and crafts of that era, which might yield suitable motifs worth adapting.

DESIGN SOURCES

Design has little to do with a facility for drawing, although sketching and painting from nature can help in several ways. It will increase your understanding of colour and form and help you develop skill in using visual language. It will also provide you with source material. But you can get ideas in many other ways. Professional designers use many sources, often taking elements – or even the basic structure – from other works, borrowing freely from paintings, book illustrations, photographs or anything else that will provide the sought-after effect.

It is very difficult to produce a good design straight out of your head, and the results, if you try to do this, tend to be disappointing. There is certainly no shame in borrowing ideas from good work in other art forms; and any time you spend studying or sketching such work will be time well spent, for in this way you will learn and understand how excellence has been achieved by others.

Opposite Above: Early Spring Garden by Janet Haigh.
Opposite Below: 19th century Persian carpet border designs.
Below: Tulip carpet by Weatherall Workshops.

When setting out to design for needlepoint, try to approach it with a fresh mind, free from preoccupations and prejudices. Never be discouraged by the badness of your first attempts. Press on; each time you reach a hurdle and find a way over it you have taken another step on the road to mastering the craft. The subject matter of your design is one of the first decisions you have to make, but it is, perhaps, the least important. There is no subject that will, in itself, guarantee a successful design, and by the same token even the most seemingly banal object can be treated in such a way as to reveal its hidden beauty.

ORGANIZING SHAPES AND FORMS
Having decided on your subject – perhaps a scene out of your family life, a pet, flowers, a landscape or one of the myriad other alternatives – how are you to set about organizing the shapes and forms to achieve a pleasing arrangement on the surface of your canvas? If you have not already done so, you will find it very useful to look at paintings and prints, as well as natural forms, to see how good designs are constructed. Japanese prints; Persian minia-tures; the works of Matisse, Gauguin and *art nouveau* painters and illustrators are all primarily concerned with the arrangement of two-dimensional shapes and colours.

One useful approach is to draw shapes for each design element you require – each one from several aspects – concentrating on interesting outlines rather than superficial detail. For instance, if you are planning a picture and your subject is a farmyard, find lots of photos, paintings, prints and illustrations of all the different people, animals and buildings that you would like to figure in the picture. It can be a good idea to spend the day drawing in your local library or museum. Copy or trace each figure in colour and cut it out. Thus you will acquire a stock of coloured shapes from which to compose your picture.

Take a sheet of paper and mark on it the external dimensions of your design. Leaving space for a border, if you plan to include one,

arrange the cut-outs on the blank paper, trying to achieve interesting spaces between them and bearing in mind that your background will also play a positive part in the design. You could also cut out coloured shapes for the background or try placing different bits of fabric behind the characters in the scene. You will begin to see pleasing rhythms occurring between some of the shapes, and as you move them around a harmonious solution should begin to emerge.

BORDERS
If you are including a border in your work, it should be considered an integral part of the design. A border can be used to pick up colours and patterns from the picture itself and, by repeating them, to balance the elements and produce a more integrated feeling. An example of this is the Mock Orange project on page 54, where the simple pattern around the Chinese bowl has been adapted and rescaled to make a border. Crisp, geometric borders around soft and delicate naturalistic pictures can effectively sharpen the design and eliminate sentimentality, as in the Daisies project on page 70, where the crisp blue and white checks counteract and balance the soft prettiness in the treatment of the flowers and background. This piece illustrates another interesting device, which is to continue parts of the central design into the border, thus preventing a wider border from becoming too strident or looking like a superfluous frame.

Persian carpets tend to use multiple borders as a main design element, often with a relatively sparse central area. The cushion [pillow] on page 58 uses the same technique. Borders need not simply consist of repeating motifs; another method is to extend the lines and shapes of the picture using a different colourway [colour scheme]. For instance, one might work a massed floral design in vibrant colours and work the outer inch or so of the picture in more muted shades which maintain the tonal values of the centre. The best solution is not always the obvious one, and you may have to try many experiments before you discover what will work to the best advantage.

Landscape by Lesley Nathan.

ALTERNATIVE SOURCES

If you don't yet feel ready to design an embroidery from scratch, you can adapt an existing picture, perhaps a photograph or postcard which could be blown up to an appropriate size, or a painting. A good way of doing this is to cut a window in a piece of cardboard and place it over a larger picture until you find an area that is satisfying in itself. Always bear in mind that you will have to make various changes, and a certain degree of detail may have to be sacrificed.

PERFECTING THE COMPOSITION

Whether you have planned your design with cut-out shapes or adapted an existing picture, when you have found what you were looking for, leave it for a while and don't look at it again until you can approach it with a clear mind and a fresh eye. Then sit and contemplate it. Try to look at it as an abstract arrangement at first. Are all the shapes pleasing and interesting? Are the colours well balanced? Look at each colour separately and see the patterns it makes as it repeats over the surface. You may find that there is a certain area of the design that bothers you for some unaccountable reason. Try to analyze where the problem lies. Is it the shape, or perhaps the colour? A change in the area next to it, or even in some other part of the picture, could be what is required. Quite often, you will have a seemingly insoluble problem in one part of the design, while finding another part very much to your liking. Unfortunately, if often turns out that the problem can be solved only by removing this favoured element. So beware of being over fond of a particular area of your design; it could be that your liking for it is obstructing your vision.

When checking the composition, pay close attention to the finer details and consider whether or not they are compatible with the grade of canvas and the stitch you plan to use. A common mistake among beginners is to try to incorporate too much intricate detail into the picture, often to compensate for weaknesses in the composition. Don't fall into this trap, for you will find the stitching tedious and disheartening, and no amount of superficial embellishment can compensate for bad basic design. Your drawings at this stage should be fairly broad with a strong composition of basic shapes and well-organized colours. As you begin to work the design on canvas, you will recognize far more accurately what it requires in the way of colour changes and detail.

THE USE OF COLOUR

Colour has often been referred to as the means by which emotion is communicated in the visual arts. Certainly everyone responds to colour and has his or her individual colour sense. Most of us need to work at developing this awareness. A clear understanding of the various colour theories, which you can gain by doing some reading, will help. Close observation of colours in nature is another good idea. Still another is to study the paintings of the Impressionists and those of other artists who are primarily concerned with colour.

The Impressionists

In the 19th century certain advances in physics made it possible to study the spectrum. The results of these studies, when published, had far-reaching effects in the art world. It seemed that when one looked, for example, at a landscape, what one saw was myriad surfaces reflecting different combinations of light waves, each in itself a pure primary colour. Excited by this discovery, certain painters – later called Impressionists – began applying it in their work. By juxtaposing hundreds of tiny dots and dashes of intense colour, sometimes almost completely without tonal interest, they managed to convey the sense of *real* light and colour – the feeling of actually being there – far more effectively than many of the more technically accomplished works of their predecessors.

Canvaswork is ideally suited to the impressionist technique, as it consists of numerous small repeated strokes – the smallest being tent stitch. Thus, areas of colour can be rendered, as in an impressionist painting, by a subtle mixing of several colours. This must be done with care. Any colour will vibrate more strongly in the presence of its complementary, but if you fill a large area with tiny dots of complementary colours, the overall vibration from a distance will be grey or neutral. However, it will be a much more 'alive' grey than that obtained by simply filling an area with grey wool.

The influence of the East

In the decorative arts, colour has usually been seen as an embellishment, a tool of design in its purest sense. Early embroideries, although often coloured in a naturalistic way, did not aim at realism in the same way as did painting. We can learn a lot about the use of colour in decorative design by looking at the arts of the East. Japanese textiles and prints, Chinese embroideries, Javanese batiks, Persian and Indian miniatures and eastern carpets of all kinds, all illustrate the decorative use of intense colour and an intuitive understanding of how colours work in relationship with each other.

Opposite: Midsummer Garden by Janet Haigh. This beautiful work was designed from colour studies of flowers made in wax crayons. The picture was worked straight onto canvas in free stitching, giving it a feeling of life and movement.

Mixing colours

Any colour of wool will always appear both darker and drabber than the same colour would in paint. This is because wool is completely opaque and has a matt finish, whereas paint reflects light. Also – in most modern painting – a certain amount of light shines through the colour from the white canvas underneath. If you want intense colour in your work, do not make the mistake of composing it entirely of strong, vibrant colours. They will fight with each other, making the piece crude, garish and, paradoxically, lifeless as well. Instead, create depth and light by mixing colours subtly and, perhaps, using a variety of stitches. Some – for example square mosaic and satin – produce a slightly glossy effect, which, if contrasted with a matt effect stitch such as tent or cross, will add highlights to the work. Although there are hundreds of different shades available, you will often have difficulty in finding the exact shade you need. Using several different shades together in your needle adds to your range and also gives greater depth to the colour. Even in a simple geometric pattern this technique can lift the design out of the ordinary. Look at the geometric background to the duck on page 75. Without the gradation of tone, and the mixing together of strands of different coloured crewels, the pattern would be flat and mechanical. Another way to liven up a geometric design is to make the occasional 'error' – that is, to insert a different colour in a random way to break up the pattern slightly.

The butterfly wallhanging (right) is another example of a basically geometric design which transcends the mechanical by careful juxtaposition of colours. The very muted and limited colour range is in shades of brown through to cream, with a soft blue introduced in the central design, and paradoxically it both conceals and enhances the geometry, by cutting across the main rhythms. The butterflies themselves are treated very naturalistically but are subtly metamorphosed into abstract rhythms that reflect their forms in an impressive use of bargello. Most symmetrical designs fall apart at the centre, but in this case the ambiguous chrysalid form, which is also a mountain reflected in a lake, wholly satisfies the mind and the eye. The handling throughout is restrained and exact and works on so many different levels that the more one looks, the more one sees.

CHANGING IMPRESSIONS

No matter how much careful planning you do before starting to stitch, you will find that the design will change as you work. You will often need to remove parts of the stitching because they do not fit in with the overall plan. Colours, for instance, look different when stitched; most will look somewhat darker, particularly in a small stitch like tent, which creates many small shadows. It is also difficult to judge beforehand exactly what a colour will look like when placed next to other colours. A narrow red line stitched in a patch of blue wool may appear to turn purple. It is also difficult to visualize the effects of a particular stitch or pattern in the context of the whole design. You might sometimes find that the effects, though different from what you have planned, look better than expected, and you might change the rest of the design accordingly.

BACKGROUNDS

Background should not exist as such. In other words, do not select a motif and then just put a plain background behind it; instead, consider this area as an active, positive part of the design. If you want to use plain tent stitch in one colour for the background, try streaking it occasionally with another colour of the same tone, or a slightly different tone of the same colour. Although you will still have basically a single-coloured area, it will look richer and more alive from a distance and will provide, on closer inspection, interesting detail. For a truly satisfying design succeeds on two levels: the large scale and the small scale. The parts relate well

with each other to make a satisfying whole, which can be appreciated from a distance, while at closer range the work offers the eye richness and variety in pattern, texture and colour.

The use of a decorative stitch – perhaps combined with a slight colour variation – is a good way of making a background or large area more interesting. This can be a very good way of dealing with a printed kit, which may have large boring areas of colour, or, in some cases, schmaltzy shading. Instead of slavishly following the instructions, you can use your own instinct for colour and texture and so turn an indifferent, stereotyped design into something unexpectedly personal and interesting.

LANDSCAPE

The wallhanging on page 26 is a strikingly lively and original interpretation of a traditional theme – landscape – and a good example of how, by carefully considering all the design elements available in this medium, one can achieve a harmonious and successful result. If we take the elements one by one, we can begin to understand the means by which this is accomplished. First, the overall design is sound, the shapes and forms being well balanced, so that if we ignore for the moment the representational value of the objects we see an abstract arrangement of shapes that work together in a positive way. There are no negative areas; no shape looks accidental, and the spaces between the motifs in the picture are as gracefully conceived as the motifs themselves.

The vibrancy and depth of colour is achieved by a very careful balance of warm against cool tones, with areas of intense colour interspersed with their complementaries and with neutrals. The border, in shades of blue and green, has the effect of cooling the central design and thereby adding a contemplative mood to an otherwise exuberant colour harmony.

The tonal qualities of the picture are essentially decorative, used to enhance and add drama to the already existing 'bones' of the design. Unlike a traditional representational painting, which uses techniques of perspective and shadows to create an idea of space, this picture creates a subjective feeling of space through the ingenious use of colour and texture. The artist has also created a feeling of depth by working the border on a coarser canvas. The large-scale stitches make the nasturtium leaves seem slightly out of focus, which has the effect of apparently bringing them closer.

Finally, the use of stitches is exceptionally good, each stitch having been chosen for its appropriateness to the subject. The artist has relied on texture, rather than line, to achieve the representational impact of the work – a good example of understanding and using the essential qualities of the medium.

Needlepoint stitches offer virtually unlimited possibilities for producing variety of pattern and texture, but they need to be used carefully. Don't just mix them haphazardly to try to enliven the design. If your project is representational, try, as this artist has done, to suit the stitch to the subject. If it is a landscape, for example, consider the sort of patterns and textures that are formed in nature. A ploughed field might be worked in kelim stitch, or a distant pine forest in leaf stitch, as in this hanging.

TEXTURE AND COLOUR
If you want your work to be strongly textural and stylized or abstract, it is a good idea to work within a very limited colour range, preferably fairly light and muted, as this will enhance the textural qualities of the piece and prevent it from becoming oppressive. Conversely, if you plan to feature vibrant, contrasting colours it's wise to play down the textural variety. Of course these are guidelines intended for the beginner; like any other artistic rules they can be broken successfully once you have acquired the necessary confidence and skill.

DESIGN HARMONY
In order to judge how your embroidery is working out, you should stand back frequently and look at the whole thing from a distance. It is very easy to get too interested in the details at the expense of the whole, or just to carry on working mechanically for the sake of speed. Remember, too, to consider every element of the design as a positive one; aim to produce harmony in both colour and form.

Below: These repeating stitch patterns illustrate how interesting designs and textures can be developed.

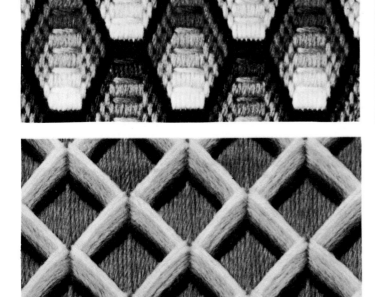

SETTING TO WORK

USING GRAPH PAPER

After you have planned or sketched your design, the next step is to transfer it onto the canvas. One way to do this is to paint the design on graph paper – a method particularly well-suited to geometric designs. Each square represents one hole in the canvas. (Note that the grid on the paper will probably differ in size from the grid on your canvas; this does not matter, so long as your original design is correctly scaled for the canvas, yarn and stitches you are using.) You then use the chart as a guide in stitching the canvas.

Working from a chart

First, draw the perimeter of the design onto the canvas, then divide the design area on both chart and canvas into squares of, say, 10 threads (lines) each. This will help you to count the stitches.

USING A TRACING

More often, you will probably want to draw the design directly onto the canvas. In this case, you first draw and/or paint the design, acutal size, on plain white paper. Next, place tracing paper over the design and trace the main outlines in black pen. Make these lines clear and not too fine. Do not put in too much detail, for too elaborate a drawing on the canvas will be confusing when you come to stitch.

Preparing the canvas

Cut out a piece of canvas the size of the finished work plus about 5 cm (2 in) on all four sides. With the help of a ruler, measure and mark the outer edges of the design onto the canvas, making sure that each line follows a row of holes on the grid. The threads may be slightly askew, for canvas, like any other fabric, may become distorted. Gently pull the canvas on the diagonal to straighten it.

Transferring the design

Place the tracing on a piece of white paper to make the lines clearer, then place the canvas on top of it so that the outline is aligned with that on the drawing. Fasten the canvas down with tape and trace the lines, which should be clearly visible through the grid. Always use a waterproof fibre-tip pen or a brush with waterproof ink or paint.

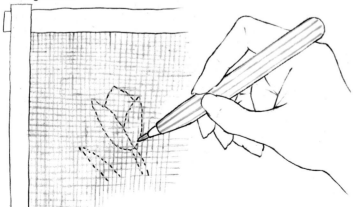

PRELIMINARIES

Before starting to stitch, bind the raw edges of the canvas with masking tape, or fold over about 6 mm ($\frac{1}{4}$ in) and sew it down firmly, to prevent fraying. Now attach the canvas to the frame if you intend to use one (see page 13).

STITCHING

To begin stitching, first make a temporary knot on the end of the thread and insert the needle from front to back in a hole a short distance away from the location of the first stitch and in the direction in which you will be working. Bring the needle up at the correct point for the first stitch. After working a few stitches – at the same time securing the end of the thread on the underside – cut off the knot. To finish a thread, run it through the back of a stitched

to begin stitching

to finish a thread

Tension

Keep the tension even. This takes a little practice, so it is a good idea to work a few sample areas before starting on your first project. It is particularly important not to stitch too tightly, for this will pull the canvas out of shape and also stretch the wool so that the canvas background shows through it.

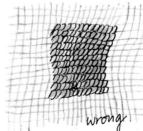

wrong

right

area, without pulling it too tightly, and trim the loose end. Subsequent threads can be started in this way, but run the yarn first in one direction then in the other for a short distance, so that the end is not pulled through when you start stitching. Don't run too many ends through in the same area, as this will distort the surface of the work. Never use knots (except temporarily in starting the work), as they are lumpy and untidy and tend to come undone. Keep the back of the work neat by trimming loose ends, or they will catch the thread you are stitching with, causing loops and tangles. Be particularly careful to keep the edges of the stitched area neat, as you will need a clear line to follow when the time comes for you to stretch [block] the finished piece.

Yarn

While you are working, the thread will tend to twist and either tighten or loosen the ply. To correct this, let the needle and thread hang occasionally and it will untwist itself.

Don't use too long a thread, as the constant friction of pulling it through stiff canvas tends to wear it down. The right length depends mainly on the gauge of canvas and type of stitch. A longer thread can be used on coarser canvas or when working a long stitch, which involves proportionately fewer pulls of thread through canvas, and so less strain on the thread.

CORRECTING MISTAKES

Should you make a mistake of any kind, do not hesitate to unpick it. If you are putting a lot of work into a piece of needlepoint, it is a pity to spoil it by being lazy about making corrections when necessary. If there are only two or three stitches out of place, unthread the needle and use it to pull them out carefully; then carry on stitching with the same thread. Do not try to unpick them with the needle still threaded, as this splits the yarn and creates a tangle. If there is a larger area to remove, cut the stitches with a pair of sharp-pointed scissors or an unpicker [stitch ripper] and discard the thread. Do not try to economize by pulling out large areas of stitching and reusing the thread, as it will be kinked and worn and will spoil the appearance of the finished work.

Repairing canvas

Be very careful not to cut the canvas when unpicking. If you do, then the best remedy is to cut a small patch of canvas of the same gauge, and, carefully lining up the threads, baste it lightly onto the back of your canvas with cotton sewing thread. Stitch over this area in the same way as the rest, working through both layers of canvas and keeping the threads in the patch aligned exactly with the grid of the main canvas. The patch will not affect the surface of the work, and the stitching will hold it in place firmly, so it will be completely unnoticed in the finished embroidery.

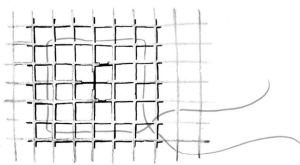

STRETCHING [BLOCKING]

When the piece is complete, it will probably be pulled out of shape, particularly if diagonal stitches have been used. In this case stretching [blocking] is essential. Even if you have worked very carefully on a frame and the piece does not appear to be distorted, the final appearance will still benefit from this process.

First, dampen the back of the worked area, using a cloth or spray (**fig. 1**). Unless it is very badly distorted, it only needs dampening lightly. This will soften the canvas, and you can then pull it into approximately the correct shape.

Using black waterproof ink draw the original outside measurements of the design on a piece of white paper. Pin or tape this onto your stretching

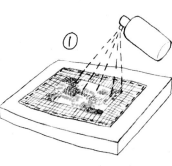

board and lay the work face down on it. Nail the work down, placing the nails at least 2.5 cm (1 in) away from the worked area, and only hammering them far enough into the board to fix them securely. First nail the four corners of the canvas into position, exactly over the four corners of the template. Then put a nail into the centre of each side. Keep on hammering nails into the gaps (**fig. 2**) until the outline is exactly right. The nails will probably need to be spaced at intervals of 6–12 mm ($\frac{1}{4}$–$\frac{1}{2}$ in). Remember as you go along that each time you pull the canvas to fix a nail in one side it will pull the opposite side too, so you may occasionally have to remove a nail and reposition it. Make sure that the canvas threads which extend from the worked area are kept straight. If they are not, the stitching will be distorted.

It may be difficult to see the drawn line through the canvas, so when you have fixed the corners in position using the template as a guide it may be easier to align the edges by placing a ruler on edge on the canvas and pulling the embroidered area to meet it (**fig. 3**).

When you have finished nailing, brush a thin layer of ordinary wallpaper paste, mixed to a fairly thick consistency, all over the back of the work (**fig. 4**). Make sure it is completely covered and that the paste is brushed well into the work. Remove any surplus paste from the unworked canvas, as it may make sewing difficult when it dries. This layer of paste will hold the wool firmly in place so that the ends cannot work loose. It contains a fungicide, which will help preserve the work over the years.

Leave the stretched [blocked] needlepoint in a warm place, but not in direct heat, and remove it from the board when it is completely dry. This will take at least 24 hours.

JOINING CANVAS

If the work is to consist of several pieces, they should not be joined until after stretching [blocking]. Place two pieces right sides together and back-

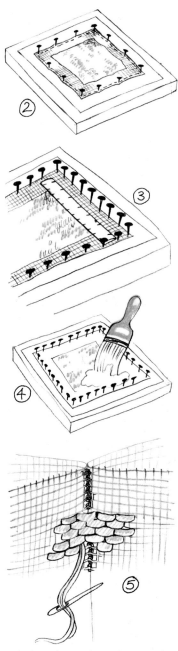

stitch, using a thread unravelled from the edge of the canvas. Be careful to align the grids on the two pieces exactly and work through the holes of the canvas. If the stitch at the edge is one that does not normally follow a straight line, such as brick stitch, parts of the canvas will show at the join. To hide this completely, first prepare the edges at the stitching stage by leaving unworked the stitches that would extend over the seam line. Then after the two pieces have been stretched [blocked] and sewn together, work the missing stitches over the seam (**fig. 5**).

Mounting and framing needlepoint

Before you take a piece of needlepoint to be framed (or frame it yourself) you must mount it, so as to give it a firm backing and keep it in the smooth condition achieved during stretching [blocking]. There are several methods of doing this, but one of the most satisfactory is to stretch the work over a piece of hardboard and lace the edges together at the back.

MATERIALS

A piece of thin hardboard the same size as the embroidery, plus a margin equal to the width of the rebate – that is, the part of the frame that overlaps the picture and holds it in place.

Heavy duty thread, such as carpet thread, and a large needle.

Panel pins

Frame

Brads

Brown paper

Tape

2 small screw eyes

Picture-hanging wire or cord

NOTE: Before ordering or cutting the hardboard it is a good idea to select your moulding, so that you will know how much margin to allow, as rebates vary slightly in width. Ideally, the inner edges of the frame will just meet the edges of the needlepoint itself – neither overlapping them nor revealing any unworked canvas (naturally, a slight overlap is preferable to a gap). If you plan to cover the work with glass, it is better to allow slightly less margin than the rebate width.

Mounting on hardboard

To mount the work, place it right side up on top of the smooth side of the hardboard. Turn one edge under the hardboard (leaving the appropriate margin of unworked canvas) and pin it in place along the edge of the board, using panel pins at frequent intervals (**fig. 1**). Repeat this step on the opposite edge.
Thread the needle with a long length of thread. Insert it in one corner of the canvas and lace the two canvas edges together, working towards the other side

and placing the stitches diagonally as shown (**fig. 2**). Pull the thread through as you go. Knot the thread at the beginning only. Remove the panel pins and with your fingers pull the lacing taut as shown (**fig. 2**), checking to make sure the margins are even on the right side.
Fasten off securely.
Repeat the preceding steps on the remaining edges of the canvas, folding the corners square (**fig. 3**).

Setting into a frame

Place the mounted needlepoint in the frame and secure at the back with brads (**fig. 4**). Cover the back with brown paper and fix with brown paper tape to keep out the dust. Fix screw eyes into frame and attach wire or cord for hanging (**fig. 5**).

Selecting a frame

Choosing a suitable frame that will complement and enhance your work requires a bit of thought. However, the decision can be made easier with the help of an expert framer, who will point out suitable mouldings from which you can choose one that suits your taste and the room in which the work will be hung. Some needlework shops offer a framing service and stock mouldings that are particularly suited to embroidery.

You must also decide whether or not you want glass. This has the advantage of keeping the work clean, but inevitably it creates reflections (unless you use non-reflecting glass) and minimizes the textural qualities of the work. If you do decide to use glass, you must choose a frame whose rebate depth will not only accommodate the hardboard, canvas and glass but will also allow a small space between the work and the glass, so that the stitches will not be crushed. A professional framer will construct the frame to provide this.

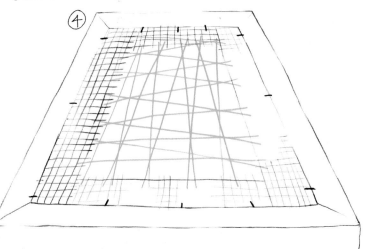

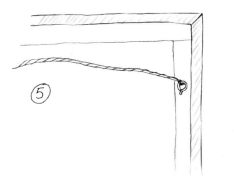

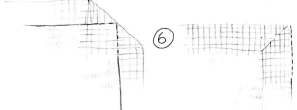

Hanging needlepoint

To back a piece of needlepoint for hanging you will need a piece of fabric that harmonizes with the work in colour and quality. Although the lining will be hidden from view, it may just be visible at the edges. For needlepoint worked in wool or cotton, a closely-woven linen or cotton fabric is suitable. If silk threads have been used, a silk fabric is ideal, but a fine cotton is quite adequate.

First turn the canvas edges of the work, mitring the corners as shown (**fig. 6**). Baste them to the worked canvas.

Cut the lining fabric to the same size as the worked canvas, plus about 2.5 cm (1 in) all round. Turn this excess to the wrong side, and baste it in place, mitring the corners. Lay the lining over the needlepoint, wrong sides facing. Baste the two pieces together around all four edges. Slip stitch the two layers together at the edges – leaving gaps, if required, for dowelling, as described below.

HANGING WITH VELCRO

If you are using this method of hanging, your work you will need:

A strip of Velcro fastening as long as the upper edge of the work.

A strip of wood of the same length.

Nails for attaching the wood to the wall and the Velcro to the wood.

Nail the strip of wood to the wall in the desired position, first making sure that it is exactly level. Separate the Velcro, and nail one half of it to the wooden strip.

Sew the other half of the Velcro to the upper edge of the needlepoint. Press the two strips together to hang the needlepoint (**fig. 7**).

HANGING WITH DOWELLING

If you are using this method you will need:

A length of dowelling about 7.5 cm (3 in) longer than the width of the needlepoint (plus another length to give extra weight at the bottom, if desired).

A length of cord

When you stitch the lining and needlepoint together, leave gaps at the upper side edges (and lower side edges if desired) for inserting the dowelling.

Sand, then stain or paint the dowelling. Insert the dowelling (**fig. 8**) and tie cord to each end of the upper length.

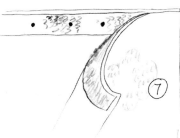

PROJECTS

Samplers make an ideal starting point for beginners. The first sampler is worked entirely in tent stitch, while the second incorporates eighteen different stitches.

SIMPLE TENT STITCH SAMPLER

SAMPLER CUSHION [PILLOW]

Simple tent stitch sampler

Size: Approximately 14 cm
(5½ in) square

MATERIALS
1 skein of Anchor Stranded
Cotton [Embroidery Thread] in
each of following colours:

Colour key
- ● Blue 0130
- ╲ Ecru/Cream 0386
- · Grey 0398
- ✚ Geranium 08
- ‒ Geranium 06
- ▬ Almond Green 0261
- ╱ Forest Green 0214
- ◦ Beige 0379
- · Beige 0376
- ✛ Old Rose 075
- ╲ Parma Violet 0109
- ╱ Tangerine 0313
- ✖ Buttercup 0292.

Piece of single canvas, 18
threads to 2.5 cm (1 in),
measuring 25 cm (10 in)
square.

Tapestry needle size 22

Indelible marker

Working the design
Draw outline of sampler onto
canvas with indelible marker,
carefully counting the threads,
and divide picture area into a
grid of 10 threads. The sampler

is worked in tent stitch throughout, using 3 strands of cotton.
Follow colour areas indicated
on chart, beginning at the
bottom and working through to
top. Each square on chart represents 1 intersection of canvas
threads, ie. 1 tent stitch.

Finishing
When the sampler is complete,
stretch [block] as shown on
page 31. To mount and frame,
see method page 32.

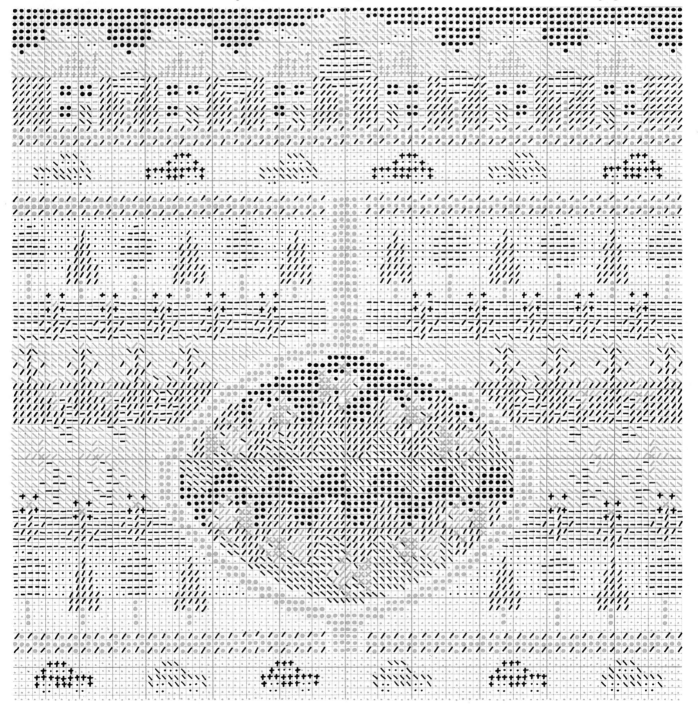

Sampler cushion [pillow]

Size: 35.5 cm (14 in) square

MATERIALS
Appleton's Crewel [Crewel Embroidery] Wool in following colours and quantities:

Colour key
7 skeins Off White 992
5 skeins Brilliant White 991
3 skeins Heraldic Gold 841
3 skeins Custard 851.

Piece of single canvas, 12 threads to 2.5 cm (1 in), measuring 38 cm (15 in) square.

Tapestry needle size 20

Very light-coloured waterproof ink.

0.40 m (½ yd) heavy woven linen in natural colour.

Sewing thread to match

30.5 cm (12 in) zipper

Cushion pad [pillow form] 40.5 cm (16 in) square

Working the design
The needlepoint design measures 28 cm (11 in) square. Mark this outline on canvas (along rows of holes, not threads) with very light ink or basting stitches in sewing thread. Mark centre point of canvas. Fill in areas of different stitches as indicated on chart, beginning with central cross stitch square and working outwards. Leave tent stitch background until last.

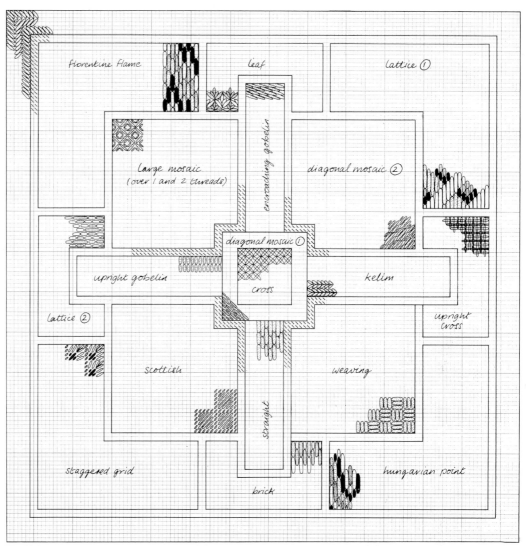

Finishing
When sampler is complete, stretch [block] to 28 cm (11 in) square as shown on page 31.

To make front panel of cushion, cut out 4 trapezoid strips along grain of linen, using **fig. 1** as a guide and adding 1 cm (⅜ in) all around for seams. Attach these strips to needlepoint by placing right sides together, basting and machining carefully along edge of embroidery (**fig. 2**)

Turn back strips, leaving canvas flat underneath. Press diagonal folds at corners of strips, baste and machine along folds (**fig. 3**).

Make up cushion back from linen to same size as front, inserting zipper about 7.5 cm (3 in) from top (**fig. 4**).

Place front and back panels right sides together, baste and machine stitch all around. Turn cover right side out and insert cushion pad [pillow form].

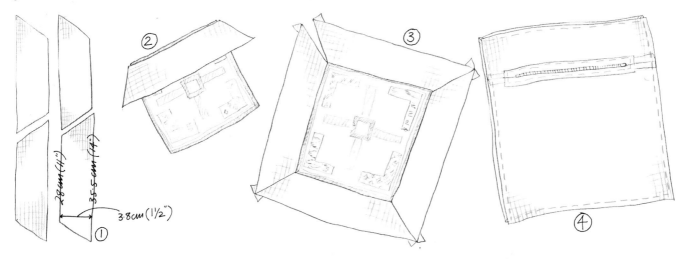

28 cm (11")
35.5 cm (14")
3.8 cm (1½")
①

②

③

④

LANDSCAPE BELT
GEOMETRIC BELT

A needlepoint belt is an excellent idea for a first project. If you decide to plan your own design, you will find that simple repeating floral patterns work well. Very effective geometric designs can also be adapted from carpet borders (see page 25). Alternatively, you may wish to make up these designs in your own choice of colours to provide the finishing touch to a simple but sophisticated dress.

Landscape belt

Size: Length as required × 3.8 cm (1½ in) wide

MATERIALS

1 skein of Appleton's Crewel [Crewel Embroidery] Wool in each of 10 following colours:

Colour key (mixtures used where indicated)

- **B** Sky Blue 562
- **P** Putty Groundings 989
- (1 strand)/Sky Blue 562 (3 strands)
- **W** White 991
- **E** Elephant Grey 971 (3 strands)/Flame Red 202 (1 strand)
- **F** Flame Red 202 (2 strands)/Elephant Grey 971 (2 strands)
- **L** Early English Green 541
- **G** Early English Green 544
- **C** Chocolate 184
- **D** Drab Green 331
- **R** Grass Green 251 (2 strands)/Drab Green 331 (2 strands)

Piece of single canvas, 12 threads to 2.5 cm (1 in), at least 7.5 cm (3 in) wide and 10 cm (4 in) longer than required length of finished belt.

Tapestry needle size 20

5 cm (2 in) wide strip of bias-cut calico [unbleached muslin] for backing.

Sewing thread to match calico [unbleached muslin].

3.8 cm (1½ in) buckle

Working the design

The chart shows a 30.5 cm (12 in) pattern which is repeated from arrow to required length. Each square represents 1 canvas thread. Work design in random straight stitch, filling in areas of colour according to key given. A double line of tent stitch is worked at each end for strength.

Use 4 strands of yarn for straight stitch and 3 strands of yarn for tent stitch.

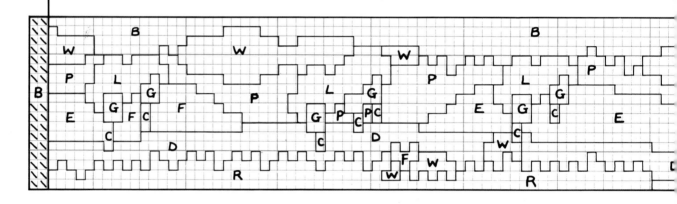

Geometric belt

Size: 3.8 × 63 cm (1½ in × 24¾ in)

MATERIALS

1 skein of Appleton's Tapestry Wool in each of following colours:

Colour key

- **F** Flesh Tints 701
- **C** Coral 861
- **B** Biscuit Brown 764
- **D** Drab Green 331
- **G** Early English Green 541
- **T** Terra Cotta 121
- **M** Mid Blue 152

Piece of single canvas, 12 threads to 2.5 cm (1 in), at least 7.5 cm (3 in) wide and 73.5 cm (29 in) long.

Tapestry needle size 20

Bias-cut calico [unbleached muslin] 5 × 64 cm (2 × 25¼ in).

Sewing thread to match calico [unbleached muslin].

Narrow leather thonging 100 cm (40 in) long.

Working the design

The chart shows half the length of belt. The pattern is symmetrical about the centre. The upper and lower halves of belt also form mirror images, as shown on the chart.

The design is worked in tent stitch and satin stitch in varying widths and slanting in both directions as indicated on chart. Each square on the chart represents 1 intersection of canvas threads.

Use a single thickness of tapestry wool throughout.

Finishing

It will probably be sufficient to stretch [block] work lengthways only. Do not paste.

When dry, trim canvas to 2 cm (¾ in) along each long side and 2.5 cm (1 in) at short ends. Turn back sides and baste down. Turn back short ends and sew down firmly.

Cut leather thonging into 4 lengths and pierce about 6 holes in first 3.8 cm (1½ in) of each piece. Sew pierced ends of thonging onto back of canvas, placing 2 lengths at each short edge.

Fold back 6 mm (¼ in) all around calico [unbleached muslin] strip and slip stitch neatly to back of belt, wrong sides together, enclosing the stitched ends of thonging.

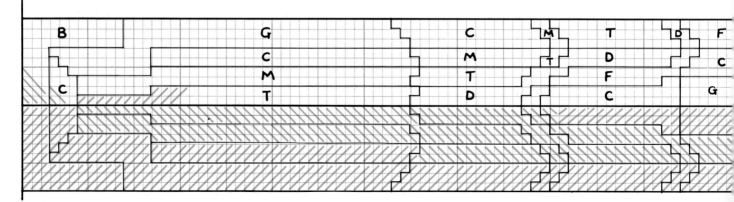

Finishing

It will probably be sufficient to stretch [block] work lengthways only. Do not paste. When dry, trim canvas to 2 cm ($\frac{3}{4}$ in) along each long side and 2.5 cm (1 in) at short ends. Turn back sides and baste down. Turn back short ends, inserting buckle in one end, and sew down. Fold back 6 mm ($\frac{1}{4}$ in) all around calico [unbleached muslin] strip and slip stitch to back of belt.

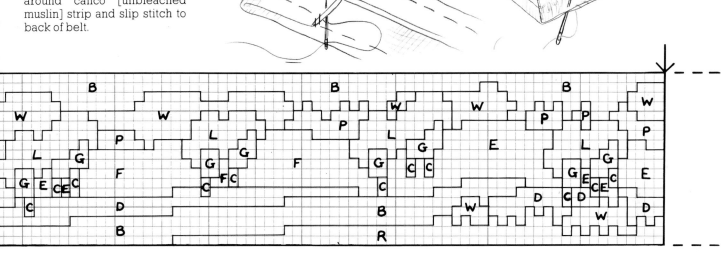

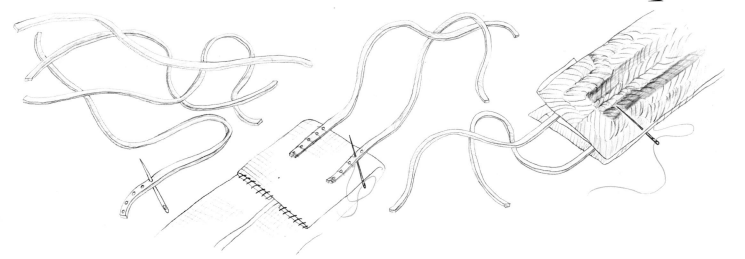

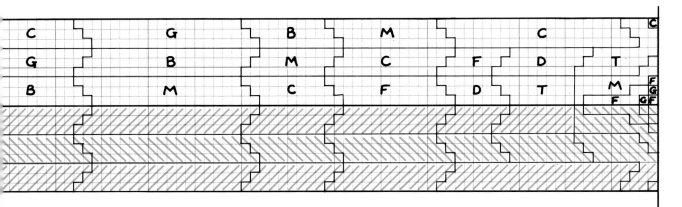

VICTORIA TERRACE

For this project we have taken a section from an original design which combines knitting and machine embroidery with needlepoint. The detail above can be worked entirely in needlepoint using tent stitch, horizontal straight stitch and French knots. Step-by-step instructions for French knots are given on page 45. To create additional texture, the creeper on the wall could be worked in leaf stitch.

Victoria terrace

Size: Approximately 18.5 × 17 cm (7 × 6½ in)

MATERIALS

1 skein of Anchor Stranded Cotton [Embroidery Thread] in each of following colours (except where otherwise indicated):

Colour key

B Cobalt Blue 0130 (2 skeins)
W White 0402 (2 skeins)
/ Chestnut 0349
\ Grey 0397
● Grey 0398
+ Indigo 0127
+ Buttercup 0298
/ Buttercup 0293
· Muscat Green 0279
◡ Muscat Green 0281
◗ Moss Green 0269
– Terra Cotta 0341
● Beige 0379
\ Beige 0376
× Linen 0391
   Coffee 0380

1 skein of Anchor Tapisserie [Tapestry] Wool in each of following colours (except where otherwise indicated):

Colour key

⬭ Slate Grey 0848 (2 skeins)
⬚ Peach 0336 (2 skeins)
⬚ Rose 0895 (2 skeins)
● Chocolate 0359
   Pale Green 0264
   Bright Green 0265
   Wood Green 0266
   Dark Green 0268
   Moss Green 0269

Piece of single canvas, 18 threads to 2.5 cm (1 in), measuring 25 cm (10 in) square.

Tapestry needle size 22

Indelible marker

Working the design

Draw outline of picture onto canvas with indelible marker, carefully counting the threads. Mark a few more guide lines, ie. windows, doors, sky (see diagram below).

Following stitch and colour key on chart, begin stitching tent stitch areas first, using 3 strands of stranded cotton. Each square on chart represents 1 tent stitch.

Then fill in background bricks and tiles with tapisserie [tapestry] wool using horizontal straight stitches to form a brick-like pattern as on chart.

Finally work hedges in French knots, using tapisserie [tapestry] wool. They are worked in five shades of green ranging from Moss Green through to Pale Green.

Finishing

When work is complete, stretch [block] to correct size as shown on page 31. To frame the picture, see method on page 32.

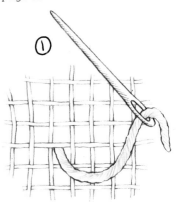

FRENCH KNOTS

1 Draw the thread through to the front of the canvas.

2 Twist the needle several times round the thread and insert back into the canvas.

3 Completed French knots.

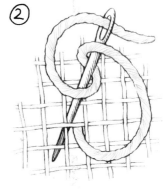

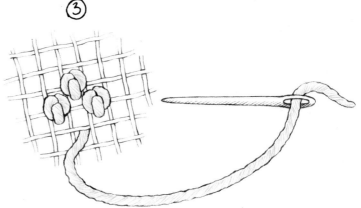

MIRROR FRAMES

Landscape mirror frame

Size: Outside measurement 16.5 × 22 cm (6½ × 8¾ in); inside measurement 10 × 14.5 cm (4 × 5¾ in).

MATERIALS
1 skein of Appleton's Crewel [Crewel Embroidery] Wool in each of following colours:

Colour key
W   White 991
O   Off White 992
P   Putty Groundings 989
F   Flesh Tints 701
R   Flame Red 202
S   Sky Blue 561
C   Bright China Blue 741
D   Drab Green 331
G   Grey Green 351
N   Grey Green 355
Y   Custard Yellow 851
B   Biscuit Brown 763
H   Chocolate 185

Piece of single canvas, 12 threads to 2.5 cm (1 in), measuring 23 × 33 cm (9 × 13 in).

Tapestry needle size 20

Indelible marker

Piece of mirror glass at least 11 × 15 cm (4¼ × 6 in), 2 mm (⅛ in) thick.

Piece of cardboard 16.5 × 22 cm (6½ × 8¾ in), 2 mm (⅛ in) thick.

4 strips of 1 cm (⅜ in) thick wood: one measuring 4.5 × 16.5 cm (1¾ × 6½ in); one measuring 3.2 × 16.5 cm (1¼ × 6½ in); two measuring 3.2 × 14.5 cm (1¼ × 5¾ in).

Piece of hardboard 16.5 × 22 cm (6½ × 8¾ in); plus piece 9 × 15.5 cm (3½ × 6 in) for strut.

2 cork tiles 23 cm (9 in) square.

Picture hinge

PVA adhesive [white glue]

Wood glue

Panel pins

Split pins

Hacksaw

Stanley [cutting] knife

Metal ruler

Working the design

Draw outer and inner edges of frame onto canvas with indelible marker, carefully counting the threads – outside measurements 22 cm × 16.5 cm ($8\frac{3}{4}$ × $6\frac{1}{2}$ in), inside measurements 14.5 × 10 cm ($5\frac{3}{4}$ × 4 in). Straight stitches are used throughout, including upright Gobelin and random straight stitch. Work design according to colour areas shown on chart, on which 1 square represents 1 canvas thread. Where 2 letters are shown in a colour area, 2 colours of yarn are mixed, ie. 2 strands of each. Use 4 strands of crewel wool throughout.

Finishing

When the work is complete, stretch [block] to correct size. The mirror and frame are assembled in the order shown in **fig. 1**. First make wooden frame to same dimensions as needlepoint, using wood glue and panel pins.

Trim outer and inner edges of canvas to 1.3 cm ($\frac{1}{2}$ in), clipping diagonally into inside and out-side corners. Fold back excess canvas and glue down with PVA [white glue]. When dry, glue needlepoint to wooden frame with PVA [white glue].

Cut a window in the 2 mm ($\frac{1}{8}$ in) cardboard exactly the same size as mirror. Slot mirror into cardboard.

Fix hinge bar to rectangle of hardboard with split pins as in **fig. 2**. Glue hardboard to card-board and mirror with wood glue. Attach wooden frame to cardboard with wood glue and hammer a panel pin through each corner.

Cut a piece of cork tile 16.5 × 22 cm ($6\frac{1}{2}$ × $8\frac{3}{4}$ in) with a small window for hinge as in **fig. 3**. Glue to back of hardboard with wood glue. Then finish outside and inside edges of complete frame with strips of cork tile, using wood glue. Exact measurements should be taken for these at this stage [step] rather than cutting them in advance. Cut hardboard strut to shape as in **fig. 4** and fit hinge plate with split pins. Push hinge plate onto bar.

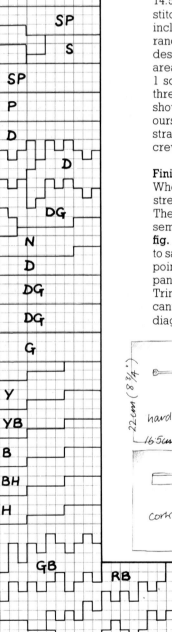

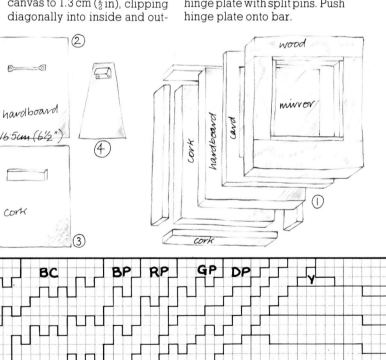

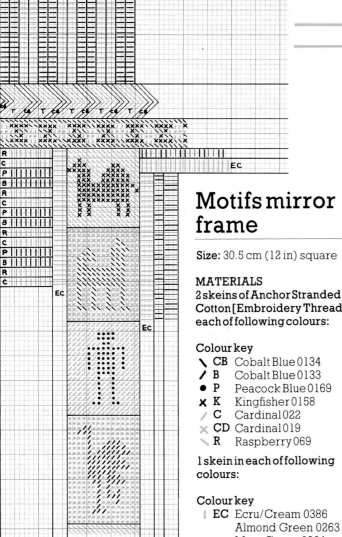

Motifs mirror frame

Size: 30.5 cm (12 in) square

MATERIALS
2 skeins of Anchor Stranded Cotton [Embroidery Thread] in each of following colours:

Colour key

\	CB	Cobalt Blue 0134
/	B	Cobalt Blue 0133
●	P	Peacock Blue 0169
✗	K	Kingfisher 0158
/	C	Cardinal 022
✕	CD	Cardinal 019
\	R	Raspberry 069

1 skein in each of following colours:

Colour key

	EC	Ecru/Cream 0386
		Almond Green 0263
		Moss Green 0264
●	T	Turkey Red 047

Piece of single canvas, 18 threads to 2.5 cm (1 in), measuring 35 cm (14 in) square.

Tapestry needle size 22

Indelible marker

Piece of mirror glass 30.5 cm (12 in) square.

Piece of blockboard 30.5 cm (12 in) square, approx. 1.5 cm (⅝ in) thick.

2 eyelet hooks

PVA adhesive [white glue]

Wood glue

Piece of pink hessian 34 × 28 cm (13½ × 11 in).

Piece of stiff card [cardboard] 30.5 cm (12 in) square.

Working the design
Draw outline of frame onto canvas with indelible marker, carefully counting the threads (220 on each side). Then mark inner edge, counting 37 threads in from outer edge. Also draw in a few guide lines for the different borders.
The design is worked in horizontal and vertical upright Gobelin stitch, satin stitch and tent stitch. Begin stitching from inner edges, following stitch and colour key on chart. All satin stitch and upright Gobelin areas are worked with 6 strands of cotton; all tent stitch areas with 3 strands of cotton.

Finishing
When work is complete, stretch [block] to size as shown on page 31.
Trim outer canvas edge to 1.5 cm (⅝ in).

From centre of stiff card, cut a 19.5 cm (7¾ in) square. From centre of embroidered frame, cut a 16.5 cm (6½ in) square, leaving border of unworked canvas approximately 1.5 cm (⅝ in). Clip diagonally into inner and outer corners.
Glue embroidered frame over card using PVA [white glue]. Glue back of mirror glass to blockboard with wood glue. Cut 4 strips of hessian 34 × 7 cm (13½ × 2¾ in). Using PVA [white glue], glue hessian over edges of mirror and blockboard; tucking in raw edges at corners. Then glue frame to mirror with wood glue and place beneath heavy weight until glue is completely dry. Screw 2 eyelet hooks into back of blockboard, and the mirror is ready to hang.

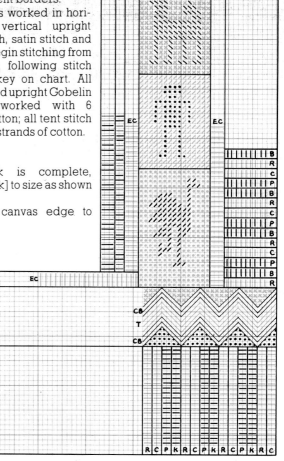

cut away centre area

1.5 cm (⅝")

31 threads

clip

220 threads

1.5 cm (⅝")

CHAIR SEAT COVER

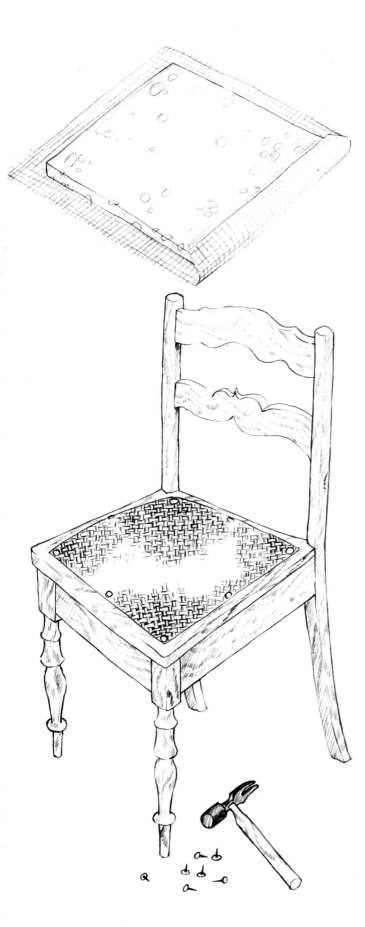

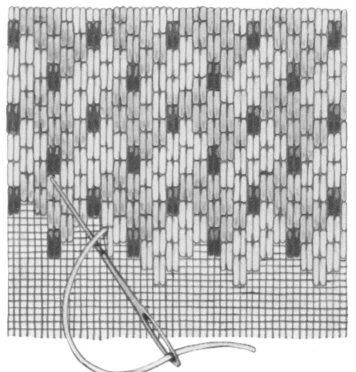

Chair seat cover

Size: Size of needlepoint will depend on size of chair seat.

MATERIALS
Anchor Pearl Cotton No. 5 in following colours:

Green 0242
Red 047
Yellow 0298

Piece of single canvas, 22 threads to 2.5 cm (1 in), measuring 10 cm (4 in) larger all around than chair seat.

Tapestry needle size 22

Padding material

Copper furniture [upholstery] nails

Working the design
Measure chair seat and cut out a paper pattern the same shape but 2 cm ($\frac{3}{4}$ in) larger all around. Draw this shape onto canvas with indelible marker. Mark centre point and begin stitching here. The design is worked in a variation of vertical brick stitch over 4 threads of canvas. Follow stitch diagram above, and repeat pattern until embroidery covers the area, marked.

Finishing
Press needlepoint gently on wrong side, using a damp cloth. Place needlepoint over padding and turn in edges of unworked canvas. Fix needlepoint to chair edges with furniture [upholstery] nails.
First hammer a nail into centre of all 4 edges. Then secure the 4 corners (opposite corners, one after the other).
Take care that the canvas lies straight and does not pull out of shape. Hammer in remaining nails about 1.5 cm ($\frac{5}{8}$ in) apart.

Pansies

Size: 25.5 × 19.5 cm (10 × 7¾ in)

MATERIALS

1 skein of Appleton's Crewel [Crewel Embroidery] Wool in each of following colours:

Colour key

A Dull Rose Pink 148
B Bright Rose Pink 948
C Royal Blue 825
D Bright Terra Cotta 225
E Bright China Blue 743
F Coral 866
G Coral 865
H Coral 862
I Bright Rose Pink 945
J Fuchsia 802
K Orange Red 446
L Bright Mauve 454
M Cornflower 463
P Bright Yellow 551
Q Bright Yellow 556
T Leaf Green 421
U Leaf Green 423
V Signal Green 431
W Grass Green 254
X Bright Peacock Blue 832
Y Honeysuckle Yellow 695
Z Drab Green 333
■ Purple 106/Black 993
AY Autumn Yellow 472

Piece of single canvas, 13 threads to 2.5 cm (1 in), measuring 35.5 × 30.5 cm (14 × 12 in).

Tapestry needle size 20

Indelible marker

Working the design

Draw main border outlines onto canvas with indelible marker, carefully counting the threads. Divide picture into grid of 10 threads.

The main design is worked in random straight stitch, the flower stalks and centres in tent stitch, and the background and borders in upright Gobelin stitch. Each square on chart represents 1 canvas thread for straight stitch areas, and 1 intersection of canvas threads for tent stitch areas.

Following colour key, work flowers first, filling in tent stitch centres and stalks after the straight stitch areas. Then work the background.

Four strands of crewel wool are used for all the stitches except tent stitch, where 3 are adequate. Where 2 letters are shown in a colour area, use 2 strands of each colour. Where MLJ is given, use 2 strands of M and 1 strand each of L and J. The hatching in centre of flowers represents tent stitch centre, consisting of an area of Bright Yellow 556 surrounding a patch of Bright Yellow 551.

Finishing

Stretch [block] to correct size. The needlepoint can be mounted and framed or used to make an evening bag (see following instructions).

Evening Bag

MATERIALS

39 × 25.5 cm (15½ × 10 in) black velvet

60 × 25.5 cm (24 × 10 in) black lining fabric

60 × 25.5 cm (24 × 10 in) synthetic wadding [batting]

175 cm (70 in) acrylic braid

Large press fastener

To make bag

Trim unworked canvas to 1.3 cm (½ in). Place velvet, right side up, on a flat surface. Place the stretched [blocked] needlepoint, right side down, on the velvet, matching the top edges. Attach the needlepoint to velvet with a flat seam along needlepoint edge (**fig. 1**). Open seam and press *lightly* on wrong side. Lay the lining fabric on a flat surface, wrong side up. Lay the wadding [batting] on top, then the needlepoint and attached velvet, right side up. Pin through all thicknesses. Machine stitch all layers together, starting in the centre and working from **a** to **b** each time (**fig. 2**).

Cut a strip of acrylic braid 39 cm (15½ in) long, place along centre of velvet and top stitch down. Cut another 25.5 cm (10 in) strip of braid and bind the short raw edge (**fig. 3**). Fold up the bound edge one-third of the length to make an envelope. Bind all around raw edges with remaining braid, tucking in ends at **b** and **c** and mitring corners at **e** and **f** for a neat finish. Finally, sew on the press fastener (**fig. 4**).

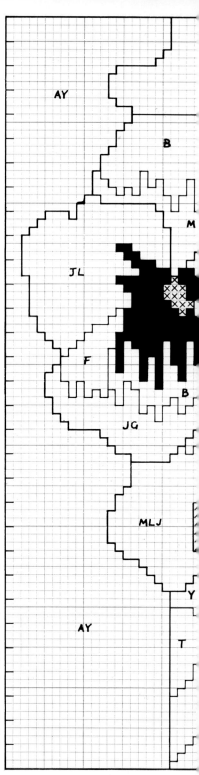

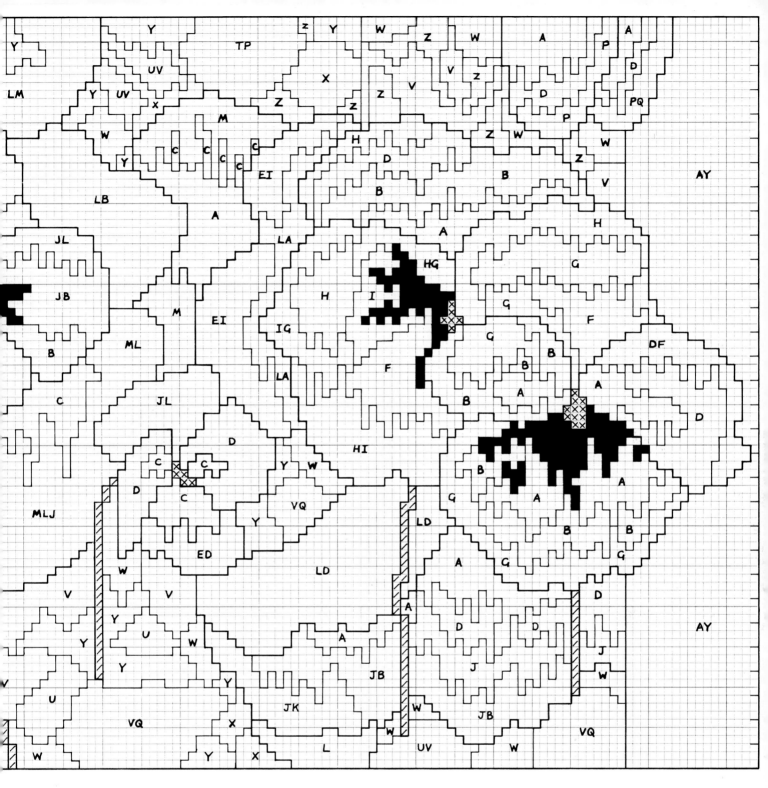

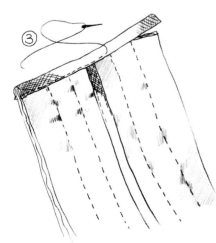

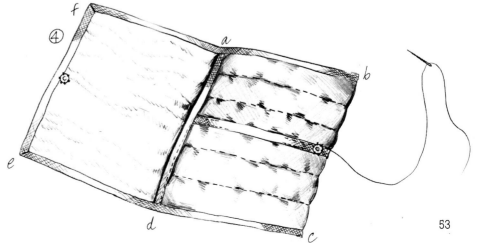

PANSIES
MOCK ORANGE

The instructions for the Pansies begin on page 52. If you prefer to mount this picture in a frame, you may like to finish the design with a border pattern worked in upright Gobelin. An effective colour scheme would be narrow bands of black and white separated by wider bands of cornflower.

Mock orange

Size: 26.5 × 28.5 cm (10½ × 11¼ in)

MATERIALS
1 skein of Appleton's Tapestry Wool in each of following colours:

Colour key
V Off White 992
◼ Coral 863
● Heraldic Gold 841
╱ Putty Groundings 989
V Leaf Green 421
╱ Signal Green 431
O Bright Peacock Blue 831
╲ Autumn Yellow 471
◣ Scarlet 504
● Sky Blue 561
◼ Charcoal 998
╲ Sea Green 404
◯ Terra Cotta 121

2 skeins in following colour:

✗ Cornflower 462

3 skeins in each of following colours:

▢ White 991
✗ Dull Mauve 935

Piece of single canvas, 12 threads to 2.5 cm (1 in), measuring 38 cm (15 in) square.

Tapestry needle size 20

Indelible marker

Working the design
Using the indelible marker, draw outline of design and border onto canvas, carefully counting the threads. Divide picture area into a grid of 10 threads.

The main design is worked first in tent stitch. The background is then worked in diagonal mosaic stitch in Dull Mauve 935. Use a single strand of tapestry wool throughout. Follow colour areas indicated on chart. Each square represents 1 intersection of canvas threads, ie. 1 tent stitch.

Finishing
When the picture is complete, stretch [block] to correct size as shown on page 31. To frame the picture, see method on page 32.

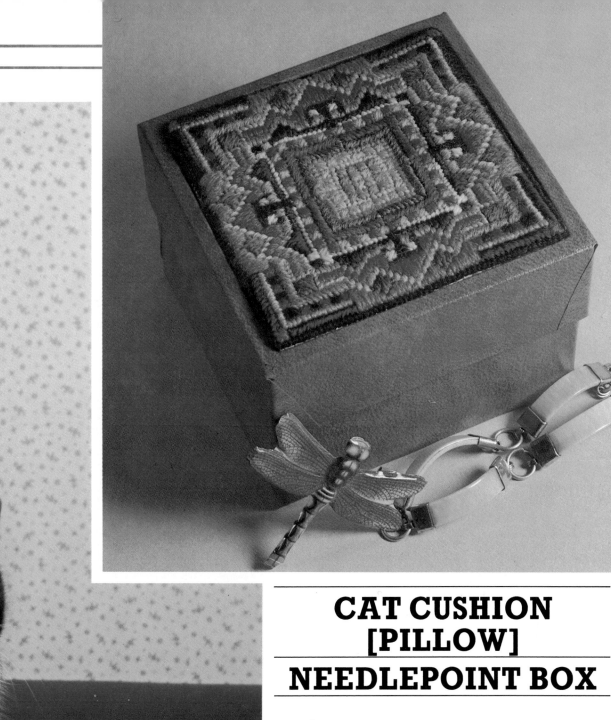

CAT CUSHION [PILLOW]
NEEDLEPOINT BOX

①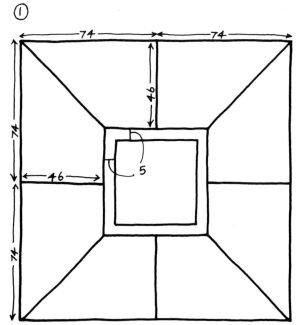

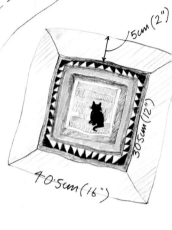

Cat cushion [pillow]

Size: 40.5 cm (16 in) square

MATERIALS

1 skein of Appleton's Crewel [Crewel Embroidery] Wool in each of the following colours:

Colour key

A Black 993
B Mid Blue 153
C Sky Blue 562
D Sky Blue 561
E Heraldic Gold 841
F Putty Groundings 989
G Flesh Tints 701
H Flesh Tints 708
I Rose Pink 752
J Biscuit Brown 763
K Mauve 602
L Wine Red 712
M Bright Terra Cotta 221
N Coral 861
O Bright China Blue 742
P Flame Red 207
R Grass Green 253
S Wine Red 716
T Bright Yellow 552
V Autumn Yellow 475
W Elephant Grey 971
X Grey Green 352
Y Dull Rose Pink 149

Piece of single canvas, 12 threads to 2.5 cm (1 in), measuring 40.5 cm (16 in) square.

Tapestry needle size 20

Indelible marker

0.50 m ($\frac{1}{2}$ yd) heavy cotton fabric in maroon.

Sewing thread to match

30.5 cm (12 in) zipper

Cushion pad [pillow form] 45.5 cm (18 in) square.

Working the design

With the indelible marker, draw basic outlines of design onto canvas using **fig. 1** as a guide (page 59). The lines should be drawn along rows of holes, not threads.

The numbers in **fig. 1** refer to number of threads crossed, ie. the number of tent stitches that could be worked along the lines. The design is worked in bands of pattern using straight and diagonal stitches of different lengths as indicated on charts. Where diagonal stitches are shown, each square represents 1 intersection of canvas threads (equivalent to 1 tent stitch). Where straight stitches are shown, each square represents 1 canvas thread.

Work central square (**cat chart**) first in straight stitches, followed by the double border in satin stitch also shown (**cat chart**).

Then work concentric strips of pattern on **border chart** from centre outwards. Begin each band of pattern from the centre of the sides. Where diagonal stitches are used, the complete pattern is reversed on the other side of the central line. Where straight stitches are used, the whole pattern is reversed in the same way, except for the first stitch which comes on the drawn central line.

Use 4 strands of crewel wool for straight stitches, 3 for diagonal stitches.

Finishing

When the design is complete, stretch [block] to approximately 30.5 cm (12 in) square, as shown on page 31, but do not paste.

To make front panel of cushion, cut out 4 trapezoid strips along grain of cotton fabric, using diagram above as a guide and adding 1.5 cm ($\frac{5}{8}$ in) all around for seams. Attach these strips to needlepoint by placing right sides together, basting and machining carefully against edge of embroidery.

Turn back strips, leaving canvas flat underneath. Press diagonal folds at corners of strips, baste and machine along folds.

Make up cushion back from cotton fabric to same size as front, inserting zipper about 7.5 cm (3 in) from top.

Place front and back panels right sides together, baste and machine all around. Turn right side out and insert cushion pad [pillow form] through zipper opening.

Needlepoint box

Size: 96 × 92 × 60 mm ($3\frac{7}{8}$ × $3\frac{5}{8}$ × $2\frac{3}{8}$ in)

MATERIALS
Very small amounts of following 21 Appleton's Crewel [Crewel Embroidery] Wools are required. 1 skein of each will be ample.

Colour key
- Sky Blue 561
- Cornflower 462
- Signal Green 431
- Bright Rose Pink 942
- Orange Red 441
- Turquoise 526
- Cornflower 464
- Bright Rose Pink 945
- Bright Yellow 555
- Bright Yellow 551
- Royal Blue 825
- Black 993
- White 991
- Biscuit 762
- Coral 865
- Putty Groundings 989
- Bright China Blue 745
- Early English Green 544
- Cherry Red 995
- Purple 106
- Autumn Yellow 475

Piece of single canvas, 18 threads to 2.5 cm (1 in), 15 cm (6 in) square.

Tapestry needle size 22

Indelible marker

Piece of 2 mm ($\frac{1}{16}$ in) thick card [cardboard], 40 × 35 cm (16 × 14 in).

'Leather-look' self-adhesive Fablon [contact paper].

PVA adhesive [white glue]

Paper, such as gift-wrapping paper, for lining box.

Stanley [cutting] knife

Metal ruler

Pencil

Sticky [cellophane] tape

Working the design
The needlepoint is worked in a variety of stitches including tent, satin, square mosaic and counted patterns of straight stitches. The chart shows the stitches as they are to be worked, ie. the grid represents the grid of the canvas.

A quarter of the design is shown on the chart which is completely symmetrical. Draw outline of design onto canvas with indelible marker, carefully counting the threads. Work design from centre outwards, following colour key given.

Finishing
When needlepoint inset is complete, stretch [block] to 82 × 86 mm ($3\frac{1}{4}$ × $3\frac{3}{8}$ in) as shown on page 31 (but omitting layer of wallpaper paste).

When dry, glue needlepoint (with PVA [white] glue) to piece of 2 mm ($\frac{1}{16}$ in) card [cardboard] measuring 82 × 86 mm ($3\frac{1}{4}$ × $3\frac{3}{8}$ in), folding excess canvas onto back. Then glue this piece of card [cardboard] centrally onto another measuring 90 × 94 mm ($3\frac{1}{2}$ × $3\frac{3}{4}$ in).

Cut out lid and base of box from remaining card [cardboard] (see measurements given in the diagrams). Score lightly along dotted lines, fold and stick corners together with sticky [cellophane] tape. Cover outside of lid and base with Fablon [contact paper], turning about 2 mm ($\frac{1}{16}$ in) to inside all around and overlapping at all joins. With PVA adhesive [white glue], glue needlepoint mounted on cardboard plate into box lid from inside so that needlepoint is proud of the surface.

Line lid and base of box with paper.

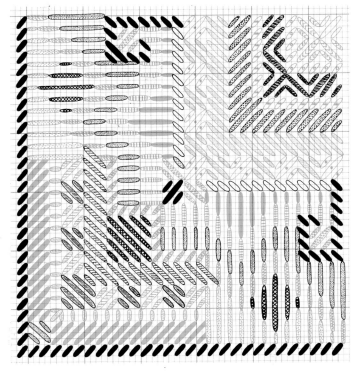

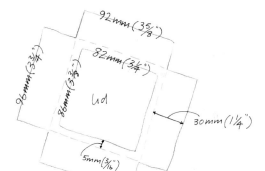

IRREGULAR FLORENTINE CUSHION [PILLOW]

FLORAL & LATTICE CUSHIONS [PILLOWS]

The attractive cushion [pillow] designs on the following pages all depend on the exciting use of colour for their success. Other shades of colour can be explored to suit your own personal colour scheme.

Floral and lattice cushions [pillows]

Size: Approximately 46 cm (18 in) square

MATERIALS
Anchor Tapisserie [Tapestry] Wool in following colours:

Colour key
Flower motif
- Ecru 0386
- Medium Pink 028
- Deep Pink 019
- Green Blue 0161
- Deep Turquoise 0163

Anchor Tapisserie [Tapestry] Wool in following colours:

Colour key
Lattice motif
- Pale Pink 0893
- Medium Pink 028
- Deep Pink 019
- Soft Grey 0158
- Green Blue 0161
- Deep Turquoise 0163
- Deep Purple 0125

For each cushion [pillow], 1 piece single canvas, 16 threads to 2.5 cm (1 in), measuring 50 cm (20 in) square.

Tapestry needle size 20

Indelible marker

Piece of backing fabric 50 cm (20 in) square.

2 m (2¼ yd) matching cord

Cushion pad [pillow form] to fit

Working the designs
Draw outline of cushion onto canvas with indelible marker. Mark centre point and begin stitching here. The designs are worked in vertical brick stitch and a variation of horizontal brick stitch over 4 canvas threads. Follow the stitch diagrams given for each cushion and repeat the motifs as shown until work measures the correct size. Do not pull yarn too tightly.

Finishing
Press needlepoint gently on wrong side, using a damp cloth.

Place needlepoint and backing fabric right sides together. Machine stitch close to edge of embroidery around 3 sides. Trim corners diagonally and turn cushion cover to right side. Insert cushion pad and sew up opening by hand. Sew cord around edge of cushion to cover seam. Push ends of cord into seam.

Irregular Florentine cushion [pillow]

Size: 28 cm (10½ in) square

MATERIALS
2 skeins of Anchor Tapisserie [Tapestry] Wool in each of following colours (the yarns have been given colour names for guidance only):

Colour key
- A Pale Jade 0203
- B Banana 0311
- C Pale Turquoise 0167
- D Dark Jade 0187

1 skein of Anchor Tapisserie [Tapestry] Wool in each of following colours:

Colour key
- E Peacock Blue 0168
- F Mid Turquoise 0202
- G Blue Green 0204
- H Leaf Green 0257
- I Muscat Green 0279
- J Pale Green 0265
- K Spring Green 0569
- L Orange 0313
- M Burnt Orange 0315
- N Pale Copper 0349
- O Copper 0572

Piece of single canvas, 13 threads to 2.5 cm (1 in), measuring 37 cm (14½ in) square.

Tapestry needle size 20

Indelible marker

Piece of backing fabric measuring 30.5 cm (11½ in) square.

Sewing thread to match

Cushion pad [pillow form] 32 cm (12½ in) square

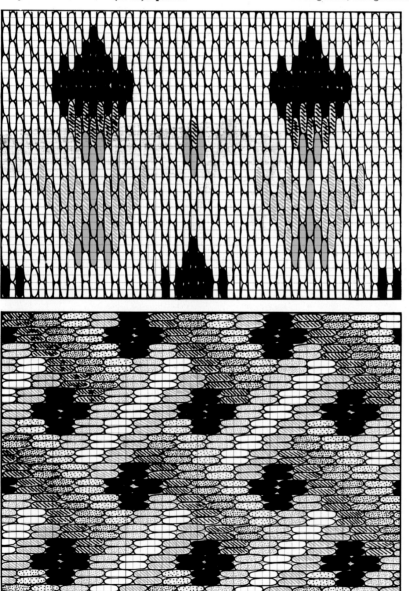

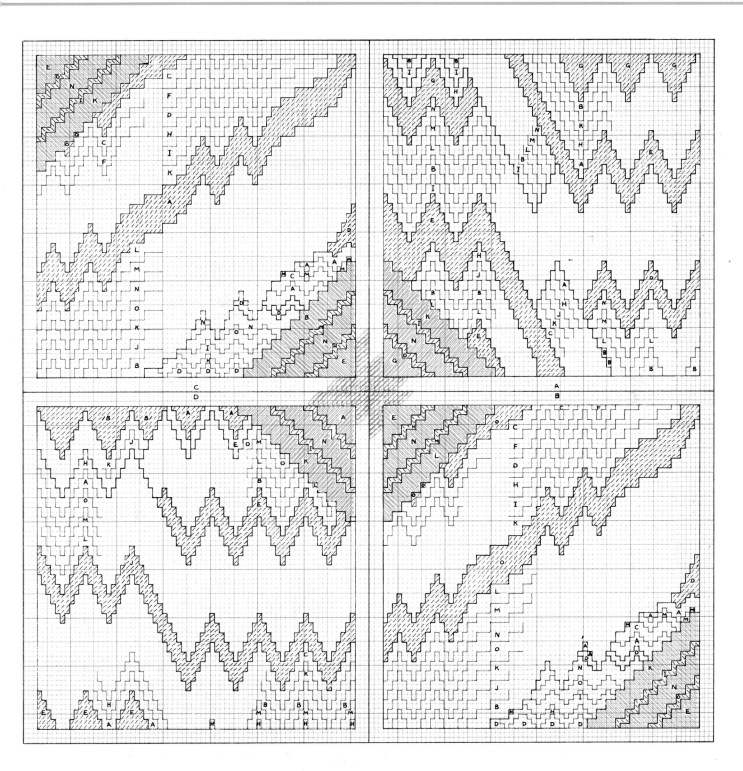

Working the design

With indelible marker, mark positions of 4 main squares, counting holes carefully. Work outlines of squares first in satin stitch, beginning at centre of cushion and following chart and colour key. Then fill in the 4 squares, 1 square at a time.

The lines on the charts represent the canvas threads.

Two diagonally opposite squares are identical in pattern but not in colour. The other 2 squares are different patterns. Work the basic lines of flame stitch or zigzag stitch first. Then add the shaded lines of flame or zigzag stitch which follow the basic lines.

Finally fill in with tent stitch or Moorish stitch as required. (Each square has 3 rows of Moorish stitch at inner corner, forming a diamond shape at centre of cushion.)

Finishing

When cushion design is complete, stretch [block] to 28 cm (10½ in) as shown on page 31. Trim excess canvas to 1.3 cm (½ in) all around, tapering at corners. Place needlepoint and backing fabric right sides together. Baste and machine around 3 sides. Turn right sides out. Insert cushion pad [pillow form] and sew up the fourth side by hand.

SPRING GARDEN
FLOWER
MINIATURES

Spring garden

Size: 21.5 × 16 cm (8⅜ × 6¼ in)

MATERIALS
1 skein of Appleton's Crewel [Crewel Embroidery] Wool in each of following colours:

Colour key
□ White 991
| Bright Yellow 551
S Lime 997
c Bright Yellow 554
S Leaf Green 421
V Signal Green 431
I Leaf Green 423
∧ Grey Green 354
\ Early English Green 546
○ Royal Blue 822

✕ Royal Blue 825
• Iron Grey 966
• Flesh Tints 702
\ Flesh Tints 708
∧ Rose Pink 755
─ Flame Red 208
✓ Wine Red 713
◣ Coral 866
✗ Elephant Grey 972
/ Mid Blue 152
○ Jacobean Green 292
▨ Putty Groundings 988
   Autumn Yellow 475

The following colour mixtures are also used (1 strand of each colour):

Colour key
● Bright Yellow 551/Leaf Green 421

C Bright Yellow 551/Signal Green 431
/ Lime 997/Leaf Green 423
+ Lime 997/Leaf Green 421
◣ Lime 997/Signal Green 431
• Leaf Green 422/Signal Green 432
─ Leaf Green 421/Signal Green 431
■ Putty Groundings 988/Elephant Grey 972
+ Leaf Green 423/Grey Green 354.

Piece of single canvas, 16 threads to 2.5 cm (1 in), measuring 23 × 28 cm (9 ×11 in).

Tapestry needle size 22

Indelible marker

Working the design
Draw outer dimensions of design onto canvas with indelible marker, carefully counting the threads. Divide picture area into a grid of 10 threads. Using 2 strands of crewel wool in needle, work design in tent stitch throughout. Follow colour areas indicated on chart. Each square on chart represents 1 tent stitch. To finish, work a border in satin stitch, using Autumn Yellow 475, worked over 2 threads (not shown on chart).

Finishing
Stretch [block] to correct size as shown on page 31. To mount and frame, see page 32.

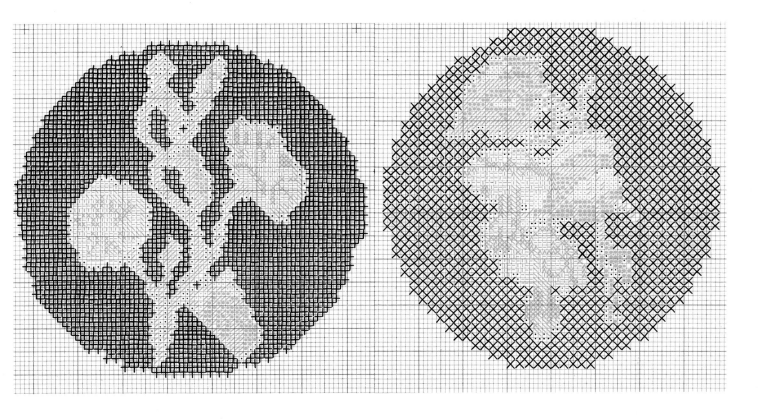

Flower Miniature 1

Size: 11 cm (4¼ in) circle

MATERIALS
1 skein of Anchor Stranded Cotton [Embroidery Thread] in each of the following colours:

Colour key
/ Forest Green 0218
● Mid Green 0845
· Almond Green 0261
| Periwinkle 0119
— Petunia 090
✕ Parma Violet 0110
╲ Violet 095

2 skeins of Anchor Stranded Cotton [Embroidery Thread] in the following colour:

✚ · 0899 [Grey Brown]

Piece of single canvas 18 threads to 2.5 cm (1 in), measuring 20 cm (8 in) square.

Tapestry needle size 22

Indelible marker

Compasses

Working the design
Draw outline of circle (5.5 cm/2⅛ in radius) onto canvas with compasses and indelible marker. The flowers, leaves and stems are worked in tent stitch. The background is worked mainly in upright cross stitch, over 2 canvas threads, and a little tent stitch. Tent stitch is used only where there are insufficient threads to make a cross stitch when filling in the background between the flowers and leaves. Three strands of cotton are used throughout. Begin stitching the flowers or leaves, following the chart and carefully counting the threads. When these are complete, begin stitching the background, working horizontally across the circle.

Finishing
When picture is complete, stretch [block] to correct size as shown on page 31. To mount and frame the picture, see method on page 32.

Flower Miniature 2

Size: 11 cm (4¼ in) circle

MATERIALS
1 skein of Anchor Stranded Cotton [Embroidery Thread] in each of the following colours:

Colour key
/ Forest Green 0218
● Mid Green 0845
· Almond Green 0261
╲ Cardinal 022
✕ Magenta 063
— Raspberry 066
| Periwinkle 0119
∧ Petunia 090

2 skeins of Anchor Stranded Cotton [Embroidery Thread] in the following colour:

✕ · Dark Cream 0887 [Dark Tan]

Piece of single canvas 18 threads to 2.5 cm (1 in), measuring 20 cm (8 in) square.

Tapestry needle size 22

Indelible marker

Compasses

Working the design
Draw outline of circle (5.5 cm/2⅛ in radius) onto canvas with compasses and indelible marker. The flowers, leaves and stem are worked in tent stitch. The background is worked mainly in cross stitch, over 2 canvas threads, and a little tent stitch. Tent stitch is used only where there are insufficient threads to make a cross stitch when filling in the gaps between flowers and leaves. Three strands of cotton are used throughout. Begin stitching the flowers or leaves, following the chart and carefully counting the threads. When these are complete, begin stitching the background, working horizontally across the circle.

Finishing
When picture is complete, stretch [block] to correct size as shown on page 31. To mount and frame the picture, see method on page 32.

69

DAISIES

This fresh and original needlepoint picture is worked in tent stitch, lattice stitch and square mosaic. The bright blue and white checks of the border have been carefully planned to add life and sharpness to the soft colouring of the flower design.

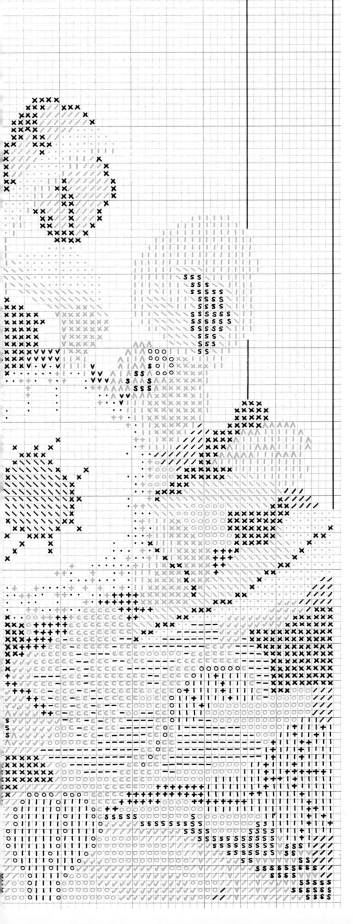

Daisies

Size: 29×25.5 cm ($11\frac{3}{4} \times 10$ in)

MATERIALS
2 skeins of Appleton's Crewel [Crewel Embroidery] Wool in Off White 992 and 1 skein in each of remaining colours:

Colour key
— Off White 992
\ Off White 992
0 Off White 992
□ White 991
• Bright Rose Pink 941
● Bright Rose Pink 942
+ Bright Rose Pink 944
o Bright Yellow 551
X Leaf Green 421
● Leaf Green 424
o Bright China Blue 746
V Coral 863
/ Flame Red 206
◣ Bright China Blue 743
I Heraldic Gold 841
C Lime 997
— Autumn Yellow 473
+ Heraldic Gold 844
/ Drab Green 331
• Signal Green 431
V Grey Green 354
I Grass Green 254
S Grass Green 253
√ Bright Peacock Blue 831
S Early English Green 542
∧ Early English Green 545

The following colour mixtures are also used:

Colour key
\ Bright Yellow 551 (2 strands)/ Bright Yellow 555 (1 strand)
\ Bright Yellow 551 (1 strand)/ Signal Green 431 (2 strands)
I Bright Yellow 551 (1 strand)/ Leaf Green 421 (2 strands)
∧ Leaf Green 421 (2 strands)/ Lime 997 (1 strand)
C Signal Green 431 (2 strands)/ Autumn Yellow 473 (1 strand)
X Grey Green 354 (2 strands)/ Autumn Yellow 473 (1 strand)

Piece of single canvas, 13 threads to 2.5 cm (1 in), measuring 40.5×35.5 cm (16×14 in).

Tapestry needle size 20

Light-coloured indelible marker

Working the design
Using light-coloured indelible marker and carefully counting the threads, draw inner and outer edges of border plus outlines of flowers which extend into border. Divide picture into grid of 10 threads.

The flowers, leaves and pot are worked in tent stitch with a background of lattice (1) stitch and a border of square mosaic. Each square on chart represents 1 intersection of canvas threads, ie. 1 tent stitch.

Following appropriate colour key, work tent stitch areas first, using 3 strands of crewel wool. Then work border in square mosaic with 3 strands of wool, and finally the background in lattice stitch with 4 strands of wool.

Finishing
When the picture is complete, stretch [block] to correct size as shown on page 31. To frame the picture, see method on page 32.

SITTING DUCKS

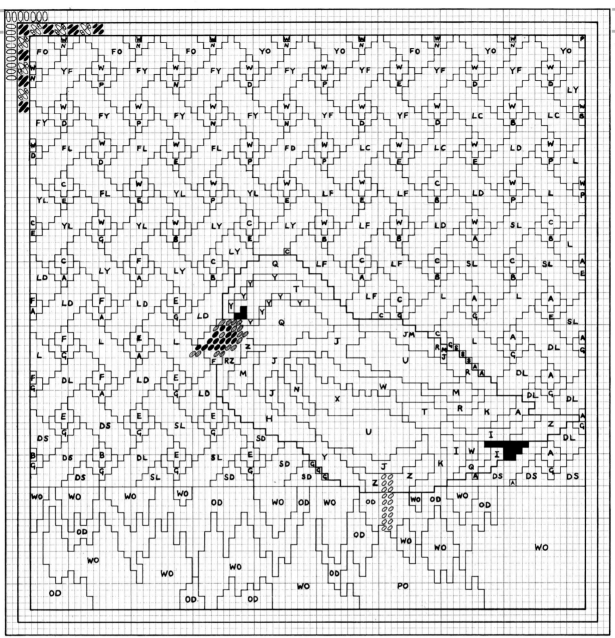

Duck with lattice background

Size: 18.5 cm (7¼ in) square

MATERIALS

1 skein of Appleton's Crewel [Crewel Embroidery] Wool in each of the following colours:

Colour key

A Autumn Yellow 475
B Sky Blue 562
C Custard 851
D Drab Green 331
E Honeysuckle Yellow 694
F Flesh Tints 701
G Grass Green 254
H Flame Red 202
I Iron Grey 965
J Bright China Blue 743
K Flame Red 207
L Leaf Green 421
M Mauve 603
N Cornflower 462
O Off White 992
P Putty Groundings 989
Q Coral 863
R Dull Mauve 932
S Signal Green 431
T Turquoise 526
U Bright China Blue 741
W White 991
X Royal Blue 825
Y Bright Yellow 551
Z Putty Groundings 986
0 Heraldic Gold 844
Black 993

Piece of single canvas, 13 threads to 2.5 cm (1 in), measuring 24 cm (9½ in) square.

Tapestry needle size 20

Indelible marker

Working the design

Draw outer edges of picture onto canvas with indelible marker, carefully counting the threads. Divide picture into grid of 10 threads.

Five stitches are used – the duck is worked in random straight stitch with tent stitch for beak and leg; the background in lattice (2) stitch; the water in random straight stitch. The border consists of a row of square mosaic surrounded by a row of upright Gobelin. Each square on chart represents 1 canvas thread for straight stitches, or 1 intersection of canvas threads for diagonal stitches.

Following colour key, work duck first (the tent stitch areas after the straight stitch). Then work water and lattice background, and finally the borders. Use 4 strands of crewel wool for straight stitches, 3 strands for the diagonal stitches (tent stitch and square mosaic). Where 2 letters are shown in a colour area, use 3 strands of first colour and 1 strand of second colour.

Finishing

When picture is complete, stretch [block] to correct size as shown on page 31. To mount and frame the picture, see method on page 32.

Duck with landscape background

Size: 18.5 cm (7¼ in) square

MATERIALS

1 skein of Appleton's Crewel [Crewel Embroidery] Wool in each of following colours:

Colour key
+ Chocolate 184
c Flame Red 208
o Turquoise 526
c Bright Peacock Blue 831
I Bright Yellow 551

■ Charcoal 998
/ Cornflower 462
V Biscuit Brown 762
– Heraldic Gold 841
+ Drab Green 331
· Early English Green 541
✗ Grey Green 354
– Dull Marine Blue 321
● Dull China Blue 924
● Dull China Blue 921
· Iron Grey 961
O Chocolate 183
□ White 991

The following colour mixtures are also used:

Colour key
V Chocolate 184 (2 strands)/ Flame Red 208 (2 strands)

\ Dull China Blue 921 (2 strands)/Chocolate 183 (2 strands)
/ Iron Grey 961 (2 strands)/ Chocolate 183 (2 strands)
✗ White 991 (3 strands)/Iron Grey 961 (1 strand)
\ White 991 (2 strands)/Iron Grey 961 (2 strands)

Piece of single canvas, 12 threads to 2.5 cm (1 in), measuring 24 cm (9½ in) square.

Tapestry needle size 20

Indelible marker

Working the design

Draw outer dimensions of picture onto canvas with indelible marker, carefully counting the threads.

Divide picture area into a grid of 10 threads. The design is worked in random straight stitch with a patterned border in upright Gobelin stitch over 3 canvas threads. Follow colour areas indicated on chart. Each square on the chart represents 1 canvas thread.

Finishing

When picture is complete, stretch [block] to correct size as shown on page 31. To frame the picture, see method on page 32.

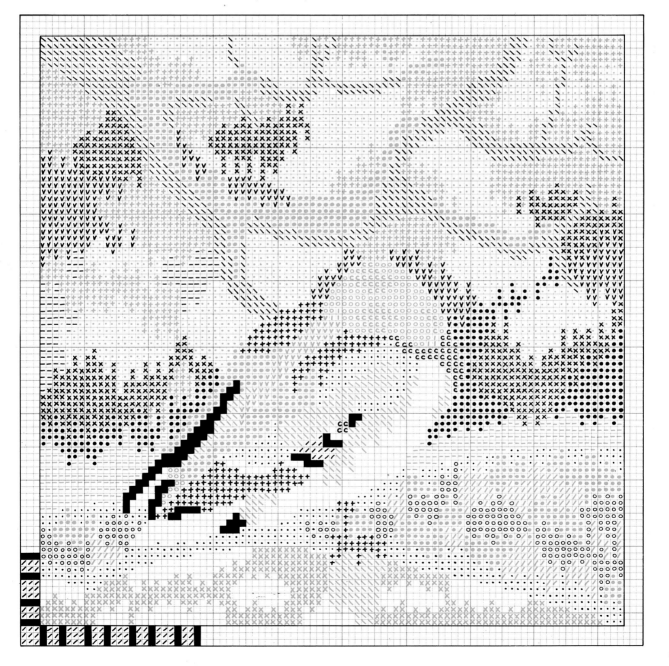

Notes for American Readers

The materials required for the projects in this book can be obtained easily from craft shops and department stores. However, the exact yarns specified for each project may not be available to American readers, and the list below has been compiled as a general colour guide. It is important that American readers assemble the colours before starting a project to be sure that they are happy with their selection.

APPLETON'S CREWEL [CREWEL EMBROIDERY] WOOL AND TAPESTRY WOOL

Autumn Yellow 471 [Soft Gold]
Autumn Yellow 472 [Autumn Gold]
Autumn Yellow 473 [Deep Gold]
Autumn Yellow 475 [Light Rust]
Biscuit Brown 762 [Camel]
Biscuit Brown 763 [Deep Camel]
Biscuit Brown 764 [Light Brown]
Black 993 [Black]
Bright China Blue 741 [Light Gray-Blue]
Bright China Blue 742 [Soft Marine Blue]
Bright China Blue 743 [Medium Gray-Blue]
Bright China Blue 745 [Marine Blue]
Bright China Blue 746 [Periwinkle Blue]
Bright Mauve 754 [Medium Blue-Purple]
Bright Peacock Blue 831/2 [Light Forest Green]
Bright Rose Pink 941 [Medium Pink]
Bright Rose Pink 944 [Medium Rose Pink]
Bright Rose Pink 945 [Deep Pink]
Bright Rose Pink 948 [Mulberry]
Bright Terra Cotta 221 [Light Tawny Pink]
Bright Terra Cotta 225 [Ruby Wine]
Bright Yellow 551 [Buttercup]
Bright Yellow 552/4 [Medium Yellow]
Bright Yellow 555 [Melon]
Bright Yellow 556 [Medium Orange]
Brilliant White 991 [Pure White]
Charcoal 998 [Charcoal]
Cherry Red 995 [Cherry Red]
Chocolate 183 [Taupe]
Chocolate 184 [Light Chocolate]
Chocolate 185 [Chocolate]
Coral 861 [Light Coral]

Coral 862 [Medium Soft Orange]
Coral 863 [Light Burnt Orange]
Coral 865 [Burnt Orange]
Coral 866 [Brick]
Cornflower 462/3 [Cornflower]
Cornflower 464 [Light Royal Blue]
Custard 851 [Tan]
Drab Green 331 [Pale Green Gold]
Drab Green 333 [Light Green Gold]
Dull China Blue 921 [Light Slate Blue]
Dull China Blue 924 [Deep Gray-Blue]
Dull Marine Blue 321 [Soft Marine Blue]
Dull Mauve 932 [Plum]
Dull Mauve 935 [Deep Mulberry]
Dull Rose Pink 148/9 [Maroon]
Early English Green 541 [Pale Apple Green]
Early English Green 542 [Light Gray-Green]
Early English Green 544 [Medium Green]
Early English Green 545 [Medium Forest Green]
Early English Green 546 [Light Forest Green]
Elephant Grey 971/2 [Soft Gray]
Flame Red 202 [Medium Rose-Beige]
Flame Red 206/7 [Tawny]
Flame Red 208 [Wine]
Flesh Tints 701 [Light Flesh Tone]
Flesh Tints 702 [Medium Flesh Tone]
Flesh Tints 708 [Medium Flesh Tone]
Fuchsia 802 [Medium Purple]
Grass Green 251 [Spring Green]
Grass Green 253 [Light Grass Green]
Grass Green 254 [Medium Grass Green]
Grey Green 351 [Light Sage Green]
Grey Green 352 [Medium Green]
Grey Green 354 [Sage Green]

Grey Green 355 [Light Forest Green]
Heraldic Gold 841 [Soft Baby Yellow]
Heraldic Gold 844 [Medium Gold]
Honeysuckle Yellow 694 [Light Tobacco]
Honeysuckle Yellow 695 [Medium Ginger]
Iron Grey 961 [Soft Gray]
Iron Grey 965 [Steel Gray]
Iron Grey 966 [Light Charcoal Gray]
Jacobean Green 292 [Sage Green]
Leaf Green 421 [Pale Apple Green]
Leaf Green 423 [Medium Apple Green]
Leaf Green 424 [Jade Green]
Lime 997 [Deep Lemon]
Mauve 602 [Medium Blue-Purple]
Mauve 603 [Mauve]
Mid Blue 152 [Medium Gray-Blue]
Mid Blue 153 [Medium Green-Blue]
Off White 992 [Off White]
Orange Red 441 [Medium Orange]
Orange Red 446 [Medium Red-Orange]
Purple 106 [Deep Blue-Purple]
Putty Groundings 986 [Camel]
Putty Groundings 988 [Beige]
Putty Groundings 989 [Light Beige]
Rose Pink 752 [Soft Rose Pink]
Rose Pink 755 [Deep Rose Pink]
Royal Blue 822 [Light Royal Blue]
Royal Blue 825 [Royal Blue]
Scarlet 504 [Wine]
Sea Green 404 [Medium Bottle Green]
Signal Green 431 [Spearmint Green]
Sky Blue 561 [Baby Blue]
Sky Blue 562 [Soft Blue]
Terra Cotta 121 [Light Rose-Beige]
Turquoise 526 [Deep Turquoise]
White 991 [White]
Wine Red 712 [Light Plum]
Wine Red 713 [Medium Plum]
Wine Red 716 [Dark Plum]

ANCHOR STRANDED COTTON [EMBROIDERY THREAD]

Almond Green 0261 [Grass Green]

Almond Green 0263 [Light Forest Green]
Beige 0376 [Rose-Beige]
Beige 0379 [Soft Copper]
Blue 0130 [French Blue]
Buttercup 0292 [Light Yellow]
Buttercup 0293 [Buttercup]
Buttercup 0298 [Medium Gold]
Cardinal 019 [Cherry Red]
Cardinal 022 [Wine Red]
Chestnut 0349 [Chestnut]
Cobalt Blue 0130 [Medium Pale Blue]
Cobalt Blue 0133 [Royal Blue]
Cobalt Blue 0134 [Deep Royal Blue]
Coffee 0380 [Coffee]
Ecru/Cream 0386 [Ecru]
Forest Green 0214 [Medium Green]
Forest Green 0218 [Dark Green]
Geranium 06 [Soft Coral]
Geranium 08 [Medium Coral]
Grey 0397 [Medium Gray]
Grey 0398 [Steel Gray]
Indigo 0127 [Blue Indigo]
Kingfisher 0158 [Light Blue]
Linen 0391 [Linen]
Magenta 063 [Deep Pink]
Moss Green 0264 [Apple Green]
Moss Green 0269 [Forest Green]
Muscat Green 0279 [Medium Olive]
Muscat Green 0281 [Deep Olive]
Old Rose 075 [Medium Pink]
Parma Violet 0109 [Pale Violet]
Parma Violet 0110 [Mid Violet]
Periwinkle 0119 [Deep Blue-Mauve]
Petunia 090 [Pale Pink Lilac]
Raspberry 066 [Light Rose Pink]
Raspberry 069 [Deep Raspberry]
Tangerine 0313 [Tangerine]
Terra Cotta 0341 [Terra Cotta]
Turkey Red 047 [Turkey Red]
White 0402 [White]
0899 [Gray-Brown]
0887 [Pale Tan]

ANCHOR TAPISSERIE [TAPESTRY] WOOL

Banana 0311 [Pale Gold]
Blue-Green 0204 [Medium Forest Green]
Bright Green 0265 [Apple Green]
Burnt Orange 0315 [Burnt Orange]
Chocolate 0359 [Dark Chocolate]

Copper 0572 [Tobacco]
Dark Green 0268 [Forest Green]
Dark Jade 0187 [Deep Jade]
Deep Pink 019 [Wine]
Deep Purple 0125 [Deep Purple]
Deep Turquoise 0163 [Deep Turquoise]
Ecru 0386 [Ecru]
Green Blue 0161 [Light Turquoise]

Leaf Green 0257 [Medium Jade]
Medium Pink 028 [Hot Pink]
Mid Turquoise 0202 [Light Turquoise]
Moss Green 0269 [Dark Bottle Green]
Muscat Green 0279 [Yellow-Green]
Orange 0313 [Orange]
Pale Copper 0349 [Copper]
Pale Green 0264 [Pale Green]

Pale Green 0265 [Apple Green]
Pale Jade 0203 [Medium Turquoise]
Pale Pink 0893 [Medium Pink]
Pale Turquoise 0167 [Light Turquoise]
Peach 0336 [Peach]
Peacock Blue 0168 [Peacock Blue]
Rose 0895 [Rose]
Slate Grey 0848 [Slate Gray]

Soft Grey 0158 [Soft Gray]
Spring Green 0569 [Medium Green]
Wood Green 0266 [Grass Green]

ANCHOR PEARL COTTON NO. 5 [PEARL COTTON]

Green 0242 [Medium Green]
Red 047 [Ruby Red]
Yellow 0298 [Medium Gold]

Needlepoint Supplies

UNITED KINGDOM
The following sell needlepoint supplies by mail order:

Royal School of Needlework
25 Princes Gate
Kensington
London SW7 1QE
Tel: 01 589 0077

WHI Tapestry Shop
85 Pimlico Road
London SW1
Tel: 730 5366

DeDenne Ltd
159/161 Kenton Road
Kenton
Harrow, Middlesex
Tel: 01 907 5476

Luxury Needlepoint Tapestries
36 Beauchamp Place
London SW3
Tel 584 0391

The Campden Needlecraft Centre
High Street
Chipping Campden
Gloucestershire
Tel: Evesham (0386) 840583

The Handicraft Shop
5 Oxford Road
Altrincham
Cheshire
Tel: 061 928 3834

Louis Grosse Ltd
Mail Order Department
Wyddial Hall
Buntingford
Herts

Ruth John
39 The Square
Titchfield
Hampshire
Tel: (032 94) 46186

Mace & Nairn
89 Crane Street
Salisbury
Wiltshire SP1 2PY
Tel: (0722) 6903
(International mail order)

Stitches
30a St Leonard's Road
Windsor
Berkshire
Tel: (95) 68068

The Silver Thimble
33 Gay Street
Bath
Avon BA1 2NT
Tel: (0225) 23457

UNITED STATES
The following nationwide chain stores usually stock a good selection of needlepoint supplies:

Ben Franklin Stores; Jefferson Stores; Kay Mart; M H Lamston; The May Co.; Neisners; J C Penney Stores; Sears Roebuck; Two Guys; Woolworth's.

The following sell needlepoint supplies by mail order:

American Handicrafts
2617 W Seventh Street
Fort Worth, Texas 76707

The Counting House at the Hammock Shop
Box 155
Pawleys Island
So. Carolina 29585

Economy Handicrafts
50–21 69th Street
Woodside
New York 11377

The Hidden Village
215 Yale Avenue
Claremont
California 91711

Lee Wards
Elgin
Illinois 60120

Peters Valley Craftsmen
Layton
New Jersey 07851

INDEX

Acknowledgments

The publishers would like to thank the following for kindly lending work to be photographed:

Sarah Windrum: landscape belt and geometric belt 38; landscape mirror frame 46; cat cushion 58
Susie Martin: sampler cushion 34; 'pansies' 54; 'mock orange' 54; needlepoint box 58; 'spring garden' 66; 'daisies' 70; 'sitting ducks' 74.
Rene Dmytrenko: simple tent stitch sampler 34; 'Victoria terrace' 42; motifs mirror frame 46; flower miniatures 66.
Mary Lawton Pick: irregular Florentine cushion 62.

The publishers would also like to thank the following organizations for the loan of the items used in photography:

title page: **Royal School of Needlework** (needlepoint frame).
pages 10–11: **Royal School of Needlework** (all materials and equipment).
pages 42–43: **Design Council** (china houses).
pages 46–47: **Graham and Green** (flowers and china pots).
pages 54–55: **Graham and Green** (flowers).
pages 74–75: **Caroline Watts** (flying ducks); **Graham and Green** (flowers and sitting ducks).

Photography by: **Theo Bergström** endpapers; **Camera Press** 50, 51, 62–3; **J & P Coates** 29; **Cooper Bridgeman Library** 7; **Oliver Hatch** 6, 14–21, 22–3, 34, 34–5, 46, 55, 59, 62, 66, 70–1, 71; **Sandra Lousada** 38–9; **Spike Powell** 2–3, 42, 42–3, 46–7, 54–5, 58–9, 66–7, 74–5; **Peter Rauter** 10–11; **Sotheby's** 25 below; **Victoria and Albert Museum** 8–9, 9.

Stitch illustrations by **Elsa Willson**
Other illustrations by **Lucy Su**

BACKGROUND PHOTOGRAPHY: OLIVER HATCH
FRONT PANEL PHOTOGRAPHY: SPIKE POWELL
BACK PANEL PHOTOGRAPHY: OLIVER HATCH